FIRST AID

▼

**A RANDOM HOUSE
PERSONAL
MEDICAL
HANDBOOK**

* Dr. Thomas P. Bem is Director of Emergency Services, Centre Community Hospital, State College, Pennsylvania. He received his M. D. degree from Temple University Medical School and completed his internal medicine residency at the National Naval Medical Center, Bethesda, Maryland. He is certified by the American Board of Emergency Medicine and the American Board of Internal Medicine. Dr. Bem is a fellow of the American College of Emergency Physicians and a member of the American College of Physicians.

FIRST AID

A RANDOM HOUSE

PERSONAL
MEDICAL
HANDBOOK

PAULA DRANOV

WITH A FOREWORD BY
THOMAS P. BEM, M.D., F.A.C.E.P.*

RANDOM HOUSE
NEW YORK

Library of Congress Cataloging-in-Publication Data
Dranov, Paula.
First aid: a Random House personal medical handbook/
by Paula Dranov.
p. cm.
ISBN 0-679-72930-5
1. First aid in illness and injury—Handbooks, manuals, etc.
I. Title.
RC86.8.D73   1990
616.02′52—dc20   90-8936

Designed by Beth Tondreau Design/Jane Treuhaft
Manufactured in the United States of America
2   4   6   8   9   7   5   3
First Edition

FOREWORD
▼

Preparing a useful text that addresses the common and not-so-common medical emergencies is a complex task. Too much information about too many conditions can create a cumbersome manual that is destined to languish on a library shelf. Providing a useful review in layman's terms that highlights the pertinent points without dwelling on details is the essence of this handbook by Paula Dranov. The author does not attempt to create a comprehensive resource for each topic, but concentrates on the "what are's" (signs and symptoms) and "what to do's" in various emergencies. In this manner a functional handbook has been designed to deliver the key information necessary to decide the course of action in many common emergency illnesses and injuries.

The term functional can also be applied to the organization of the text. Instead of listing emergency conditions in body system categories or by alphabetical indexing, the author has adopted common scenarios in which associated emergencies may develop. These groupings include emergencies that may occur while driving your car, when at the seashore, in the wilderness, sports-related, and while traveling abroad. There are additional sections discussing emergencies that can happen anywhere, and a "special needs section," which reviews particular problems that may arise in individuals who have underlying medical conditions, such as heart disease, diabetes, or pregnancy.

The reader is encouraged to use the book as a source for preparation for extended trips and vacations. Tables are provided to record personal demographic data, medical history, medications and drug allergies, and insurance information. The author has included suggestions for first-aid kits that suit the special problems that may develop dependent upon the nature of one's travel. Many common-sense recommendations are made. Though they may seem simplistic and obvious, as in advising carrying a supply of coins for phone use, these suggestions remind us of indispensable needs when action is required.

Certain areas are discussed in detail, particularly the special needs section, which addresses specific disease states with their associated emergencies. Diabetic emergencies and first-aid measures include information on insulin shock, diabetic coma, and hyperglycemic nonketotic hyperosmolar coma. The reader will find a number of topics duplicated under the various scenarios. This was done to allow a listing of potential emergencies within the section that pertains to an activity, and avoids the need to be referred elsewhere.

Overall, the medical terminology is kept to a level understandable by the general public. A brief glossary is provided to help the reader understand the technical terms that are used. The result is that this handbook will provide a ready source of useful information when unexpected medical problems arise.

Thomas P. Bem, M.D., F.A.C.E.P.

CONTENTS
▼

INTRODUCTION

▼

This guide to first aid away from home has been designed with portability and destinations in mind. It contains first-aid procedures for emergencies that can occur when you're at leisure, on vacation or en route. Most sections are self-contained units to be used independently of the others. The only exceptions to this rule are the first two, Emergencies That Can Happen Anywhere and Special Needs (for use when one of your party has a health problem that may give rise to emergencies requiring your help).

The pages that follow are designed to accommodate personal data about you and your traveling companions. Fill out the Personal Data pages with each person's name, address, doctor's name, insurance information. If any of you has a health problem, describe it and, where applicable, record on the following pages any drugs the person takes. You may want to make photocopies of the blank pages before you fill them in, so you will have extras on hand should more than three persons be traveling together or if you anticipate future trips with other traveling companions.

If one of your party does have a health problem that

could lead to an emergency, at least one other person should become familiar with the symptoms and correct response. This individual should know where to find and how to administer any medications that might be required.

Immediately after the personal-information data pages, you will find several first-aid report forms for use should an injury occur that may require medical treatment beyond first aid. The information could prove very useful to medical personnel. Make an effort to fill out a form whenever a serious injury occurs. If there are more than two uninjured persons present, record keeping can be entrusted to whoever is not directly involved in administering first aid.

You will find on page xxxv a description of cardio-pulmonary resuscitation (CPR), a first-aid technique that may be required in the event of an injury or heart attack that renders a victim unconscious and results in cessation of a heartbeat. It stands alone because it is broadly applicable. Other first-aid techniques with which you should become familiar—bandaging, and the Heimlich maneuver to be administered when someone is choking—are described in context: You will find bandaging under Bleeding (page 4) in the section on Emergencies that Can Happen Anywhere and the Heimlich maneuver under Choking (page 16) in the same section.

Familiarize yourself with the contents of the section describing Emergencies that Can Happen Anywhere. You may also want to glance through the section on first aid for emergencies in the car. In fact, you may want to keep this book in the glove compartment most of the time and take it with you only when the car will not be readily accessible: when you are at the beach, in the wilderness or traveling abroad.

The sections on first aid in the car, at the beach, in the wilderness, for sports-related injuries and traveling abroad are designed to encompass most emergencies that could develop in those particular settings. There are some overlaps. For instance, first aid for drowning appears in three sections, At the Beach, In the Wilderness, and Sports. You may find it convenient to mark the section you may be needing on any particular day with a paper clip so you can turn to it easily.

Each section includes a listing of first-aid kit contents that may vary depending on your destination. Some sections also contain suggested precautions that, if adopted, could reduce the danger of accident or injury.

At the back of the book, beginning on page 155, you will find an index of all the emergency situations covered here. If you need a quick reference, simply refer to these pages.

Armed with this guide, you should have readily accessible and easy-to-use first-aid information on hand wherever you go. With luck, and care, you will never have to use it.

PERSONAL DATA

NAME ....

ADDRESS ....

....

....

TELEPHONE home .... work/school ....

IN CASE OF EMERGENCY NOTIFY ....

TELEPHONE home .... work/school ....

ADDRESS ....

....

....

PHYSICIAN'S NAME ....

TELEPHONE ....

ADDRESS ....

....

....

AMBULANCE AND/OR LOCAL EMERGENCY

NUMBER ....

LOCAL HOSPITAL ....

TELEPHONE ....

PERSONAL DATA

ADDRESS ....

....

....

HEALTH INSURANCE COMPANY ....

POLICY NUMBER ....

MAJOR MEDICAL INSURANCE COMPANY ....

POLICY NUMBER ....

MEDICAL HISTORY

DIAGNOSIS ....

....

....

....

....

....

....

....

....

....

DRUG ALLERGIES ....

....

MEDICATIONS

(Clip or staple a copy of your prescription(s) to the opposite side of this page.)

DRUG ....

DOSAGE ....

DIRECTIONS FOR USE ....

....

POSSIBLE SIDE EFFECTS ....

....

OVERDOSE SYMPTOMS ....

....

....

DRUG ....

DOSAGE ....

DIRECTIONS FOR USE ....

....

POSSIBLE SIDE EFFECTS ....

....

OVERDOSE SYMPTOMS ....

....

PERSONAL DATA

DRUG ....

DOSAGE ....

DIRECTIONS FOR USE ....
....

POSSIBLE SIDE EFFECTS ....
....

OVERDOSE SYMPTOMS ....
....
....

DRUG PRECAUTIONS ....
....
....
....
....
....
....
....
....
....

PERSONAL DATA

NAME ....

ADDRESS ....

....

....

TELEPHONE home .... work/school ....

IN CASE OF EMERGENCY NOTIFY ....

TELEPHONE home .... work/school ....

ADDRESS ....

....

....

PHYSICIAN'S NAME ....

TELEPHONE ....

ADDRESS ....

....

....

AMBULANCE AND/OR LOCAL EMERGENCY

NUMBER ....

LOCAL HOSPITAL ....

TELEPHONE ....

PERSONAL DATA

ADDRESS ....

....

....

HEALTH INSURANCE COMPANY ....

POLICY NUMBER ....

MAJOR MEDICAL INSURANCE COMPANY ....

POLICY NUMBER ....

MEDICAL HISTORY

DIAGNOSIS ....

....

....

....

....

....

....

....

....

DRUG ALLERGIES ....

....

MEDICATIONS

(Clip or staple a copy of your prescription(s) to the opposite side of this page.)

DRUG ....

DOSAGE ....

DIRECTIONS FOR USE ....

....

POSSIBLE SIDE EFFECTS ....

....

OVERDOSE SYMPTOMS ....

....

....

DRUG ....

DOSAGE ....

DIRECTIONS FOR USE ....

....

POSSIBLE SIDE EFFECTS ....

....

OVERDOSE SYMPTOMS ....

....

PERSONAL DATA

DRUG ....

DOSAGE ....

DIRECTIONS FOR USE ....
....

POSSIBLE SIDE EFFECTS ....
....

OVERDOSE SYMPTOMS ....
....
....

DRUG PRECAUTIONS ....
....
....
....
....
....
....
....
....

P ERSONAL DATA

NAME ....

ADDRESS ....

....

....

TELEPHONE home .... work/school ....

IN CASE OF EMERGENCY NOTIFY ....

TELEPHONE home .... work/school ....

ADDRESS ....

....

....

PHYSICIAN'S NAME ....

TELEPHONE ....

ADDRESS ....

....

....

AMBULANCE AND/OR LOCAL EMERGENCY

NUMBER ....

LOCAL HOSPITAL ....

TELEPHONE ....

PERSONAL DATA

ADDRESS ....

....

....

HEALTH INSURANCE COMPANY ....

POLICY NUMBER ....

MAJOR MEDICAL INSURANCE COMPANY ....

POLICY NUMBER ....

MEDICAL HISTORY

DIAGNOSIS ....

....

....

....

....

....

....

....

....

DRUG ALLERGIES ....

....

MEDICATIONS

(Clip or staple a copy of your prescription(s) to the opposite side of this page.)

DRUG ....

DOSAGE ....

DIRECTIONS FOR USE ....

....

POSSIBLE SIDE EFFECTS ....

....

OVERDOSE SYMPTOMS ....

....

....

DRUG ....

DOSAGE ....

DIRECTIONS FOR USE ....

....

POSSIBLE SIDE EFFECTS ....

....

OVERDOSE SYMPTOMS ....

....

PERSONAL DATA

DRUG ....

DOSAGE ....

DIRECTIONS FOR USE ....

....

POSSIBLE SIDE EFFECTS ....

....

OVERDOSE SYMPTOMS ....

....

....

DRUG PRECAUTIONS ....

....

....

....

....

....

....

....

....

IRST-AID REPORT FORM

(Make photocopies of this form so that a supply of blanks will always be available.)

VICTIM'S NAME ....

ADDRESS ....

....

....

NOTIFY (Name) ....

RELATIONSHIP ....

ADDRESS ....

....

TELEPHONE ....

DATE ....

TIME OF INJURY ....

DESCRIPTION OF INJURIES ....

....

....

....

....

....

FIRST AID ADMINISTERED ....

....

....

....

....

....

....

....

....

....

....

....

....

....

....

....

....

....

....

....

FIRST-AID REPORT FORM

VICTIM'S NAME ....

ADDRESS ....

....

....

NOTIFY (Name) ....

RELATIONSHIP ....

ADDRESS ....

....

TELEPHONE ....

DATE ....

TIME OF INJURY ....

DESCRIPTION OF INJURIES ....

....

....

....

....

....

....

....

....

FIRST-AID REPORT FORM

FIRST AID ADMINISTERED ....
....
....
....
....
....
....
....
....
....
....
....
....
....
....
....
....
....
....
....

FIRST-AID REPORT FORM

VICTIM'S NAME ....

ADDRESS ....

....

....

NOTIFY (Name) ....

RELATIONSHIP ....

ADDRESS ....

....

TELEPHONE ....

DATE ....

TIME OF INJURY ....

DESCRIPTION OF INJURIES ....

....

....

....

....

....

....

....

FIRST-AID REPORT FORM

FIRST AID ADMINISTERED ....

....

....

....

....

....

....

....

....

....

....

....

....

....

....

....

....

....

....

....

FIRST-AID REPORT FORM

VICTIM'S NAME ....

ADDRESS ....

....

....

NOTIFY (Name) ....

RELATIONSHIP ....

ADDRESS ....

....

TELEPHONE ....

DATE ....

TIME OF INJURY ....

DESCRIPTION OF INJURIES ....

....

....

....

....

....

....

....

FIRST AID ADMINISTERED ....

....

....

....

....

....

....

....

....

....

....

....

....

....

....

....

....

....

....

....

CARDIOPULMONARY RESUSCITATION (CPR)
(MOUTH TO MOUTH RESUSCITATION/CHEST COMPRESSION)

CPR combines mouth-to-mouth resuscitation to restore breathing with chest compression to keep blood flowing when an individual loses consciousness due to an injury, heart attack or other life-threatening emergency.

Mouth-to-mouth resuscitation is required whenever a victim is not breathing.

Chest compression is added to mouth-to-mouth resuscitation *only* when you can detect no pulse or heartbeat.

The basics of CPR are outlined below but should be regarded only as an introduction to or reminder of the correct technique. Reading instructions is *not* sufficient preparation for performing CPR. You can cause serious injury if you are not properly trained. Even worse, your efforts probably will be futile (as they can be even when an expert is in charge). Contact your local chapter of the Red Cross or the American Heart Association for information on available courses.

MOUTH-TO-MOUTH RESUSCITATION

- With the victim lying on his back, determine whether or not he or she is breathing.
- Watch for chest movement, listen for sounds of breathing or place your cheek next to the victim's face to see if you can feel his breath.
- If you can't detect breathing, tip the head back and pull the chin forward so the mouth is open and tongue and epiglotis cannot obstruct the throat.
- Keeping the victim's head in position so that the airway remains open, pinch the nostrils closed. Then take a deep breath and place your mouth on the victim's. Make as tight a seal as possible and breathe into the victim's mouth twice (taking a deep breath yourself in between).
- Continue mouth-to-mouth breathing once every five seconds.

CHEST COMPRESSION

- Determine whether the victim's heart is beating by feeling the chest or a pulse (the easiest to find is in the carotid artery under the jawbone on either side of the Adam's apple.
- To restore heartbeat, press down on the sternum (the breastbone in front of the chest) at an even rate of 80 to 100 compressions per minute, stopping after every 15 compressions to breathe twice into the victim's mouth.

WARNING: If not done correctly, chest compression may cause broken ribs, internal bruising and/or bleeding; it also may injure the heart. Poor technique can also prevent the heart from filling with blood for you to pump out with the next compression.

Other CPR rules:

- If you are alone with the victim, begin CPR *before* leaving to call for help. However, do not interrupt CPR for more than thirty seconds.
- Check the victim's pulse after you have begun CPR; check again after the first four cycles of chest compression and mouth-to-mouth breathing and every few minutes thereafter.
- *Never* interrupt CPR for longer than seven seconds except to call for help; even then, don't delay resuming CPR for longer than thirty seconds.
- Keep your CPR skills up to par by taking a refresher course every two years.

EMERGENCIES THAT CAN HAPPEN ANYWHERE

▼

INDEX

ABDOMINAL PAIN

PERSISTENT, severe or worsening abdominal pain requires prompt medical attention. Fever, nausea, vomiting, diarrhea, loss of appetite, a tender or swollen abdomen, fever, perspiration, pallor accompanying even intermittent or mild abdominal pain, indicate that something could be seriously wrong. Among the possibilities: appendicitis, an obstructed bowel, an ectopic pregnancy (one that develops outside the uterus; the woman may not realize she is pregnant. See page 45). All these conditions are potentially life-threatening and will require surgery. Other possible serious causes of abdominal pain are an inflamed gall-bladder, a kidney stone, an inflamed pancreas, diverticulitis, and, rarely, a degenerating fibroid tumor (especially in pregnancy).

The following general rules apply to any episode of severe, persistent or worsening abdominal pain:

- Do *not* give the victim medication of any kind.
- *Never* treat abdominal pain with enemas or laxatives.

- Do *not* give the victim anything to eat or drink (including water) except on the advice of a physician.

The *only* exception to these rules is abdominal pain due to menstrual cramps, which can be treated with aspirin or other over-the-counter pain medications. If there is any doubt that menstrual cramps are responsible for the pain, seek medical attention.

Abdominal Pain in Children

Lack of appetite and abdominal tenderness may be the only signs of appendicitis in children.

A number of serious abdominal conditions requiring prompt medical attention can occur in infants. Crying while bending the legs or drawing the knees into the chest is a sign that something could be seriously wrong.

BLEEDING

Bleeding may occur as a result of cuts, scrapes, scratches, puncture wounds (from knives, needles, bullets, etc.). *Wounds to the abdomen or chest require prompt medical attention; surgery may be necessary.* For other injuries:

- Apply firm pressure directly over the wound.
- If bleeding is heavy, place a clean cloth (sterile gauze is best) over the wound and press firmly. Try to bring the edges of the wound together before applying the compress.
- If blood seeps through the compress, place additional layers on top of it; don't move and replace it.

- When bleeding slows, fasten the compress in place with bandages, strips of clean cloth, a belt or whatever is available. (See Bandaging, below.)
- If an arm or leg is injured, elevate it to a level above the victim's heart. Keep it raised even after bandaging.

If bleeding doesn't stop, exerting pressure at key points on the body may help:

- If the wound is on the arm, squeeze the inside of the arm midway between the elbow and armpit.
- If the leg is bleeding, press firmly with the heel of the hand on the victim's groin where the torso and thigh meet.

Never apply a tourniquet unless other measures fail. If you cannot stop the bleeding with the measure described above, follow these directions to the letter:

1. Place the tourniquet as close to the bleeding as possible. It should not actually touch the wound. Apply it closer to the trunk of the body than the source of the bleeding.
2. Use a long, flat piece of clean cloth. A tie or belt will do if nothing else is available, but cushion it with a folded cloth to avoid cutting into the victim's skin.
3. Tighten the tourniquet just enough to control bleeding.
4. Do *not* remove or loosen the tourniquet. You could dislodge clots; there also is a danger of shock after tourniquet removal. Get medical help.

Take precautions against shock (see page 26).

To treat wounds after bleeding stops (this does *not* apply when a tourniquet has been used):

- Wash your hands thoroughly with soap and water.
- Clean the wound gently with soap and water to remove dirt; rinse thoroughly; don't try to remove anything deeply embedded in or under the skin. Instead, get the victim to a doctor as soon as possible.
- Gently pat the wound dry with a clean cloth and cover with a sterile dressing, if available, or more clean cloth. Except when cuts are minor or superficial, don't apply any type of medication (including antiseptics and over-the-counter remedies) before consulting a doctor.
- Watch for signs of infection: fever, redness, swelling, tenderness or pain, pus or red streaks in the skin leading from the injury. Get the victim to a doctor if any of these symptoms occur.
- Wounds may need to be sutured. The patient should see a doctor within six hours of injury. Delays may result in increased risk of infection or inability to suture due to risk of infection.
- See a doctor for all severe wounds, when anything is embedded in the wound and if the victim hasn't had a recent tetanus shot.

Bandaging

A bandage holds a dressing in place over a wound. To apply any bandage:
- Wash your hands before touching the area surrounding the wound.
- Wash the wound itself with soap and water to remove as much dirt and debris as possible.

- Do *not* bandage a wound that has not been cleaned (it will increase the risk of infection).
- Apply a sterile dressing to the wound. Fasten dressing in place with bandage.
- The bandage should be tight enough to hold the dressing firmly in place but not so tight that it causes discomfort or impedes circulation.

Types of Bandages

BUTTERFLY: These are shaped like butterflies and used to close a cut. The narrow center part goes over the cut; several may be needed to close a long cut. They are not appropriate for puncture wounds or gaping wounds.

ROLLER BANDAGE: These long strips of muslin or gauze come in widths ranging from one to three inches; the narrowest (one inch) are for fingers and toes; wider ones can be used on arms, legs and the trunk. To apply, start to wind the bandage at a point below the dressing and continue beyond it; for example, to bandage a finger, start at the base and wind the bandage around the finger overlapping each turn slightly until you reach the tip. Fasten by encircling the end with adhesive tape. The same principle applies to bandaging other body parts; to keep the bandage smooth and neat, reverse it at each turn by twisting the top of the roll away from the direction you're going.

To bandage the jaw, wrap a roller bandage around the forehead once or twice and then down one side of the head around the jaw and back over the top of the head; circle the head several times.

SLING

COLLIN LEECH

8

SLINGS: You can make a sling from a large triangular bandage, large rectangular scarf or other square of cloth large enough to fold into a triangle capable of supporting the arm.

- Drape one of the long ends of the triangle behind the shoulder opposite the injured arm.
- The other long end goes behind the bent, injured arm and then up and over it to the shoulder; tie the two "long" ends together behind the neck.
- The third point of the triangle now lies behind the elbow of the injured arm and should be folded up and attached to the front of the sling with a safety pin.

BROKEN BONES

A broken bone may or may not protrude through the skin. Most do not. The following symptoms suggest a broken bone:

- Hearing or feeling a bone snap
- Pain or tenderness when the point of injury is touched or moved
- Any difficulty or abnormality in moving the injured area, including a grating sensation
- Swelling or discoloration
- A noticeable difference in appearance when compared to the other side of the body—for example, an injured arm that "hangs" differently from the uninjured arm

First aid for any fracture is to splint and support the bone: You can improvise a splint from boards, sticks,

SPLINT

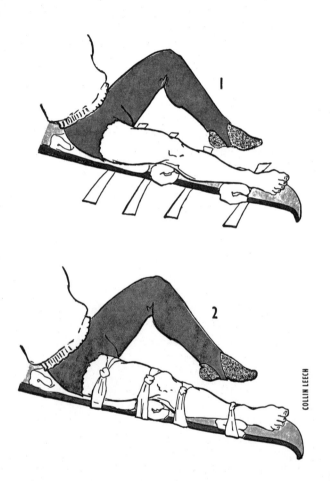

broom handles, umbrellas, oars, rolled magazines or newspapers, pillows, folded blankets, coats or jackets.

Always cushion the splint with a towel or folded clothing.

Hold the splint in place by tying it with strips of bandage, a belt, necktie, strips of cloth. Tie firmly but not tightly.

Ankle

- With the victim lying down, gently remove the shoe on the injured foot.
- If a pillow is available, wrap it around the foot and tie it in place. If not, use a folded blanket, jacket, coat or whatever thick article of clothing is handy. The idea is to protect and immobilize the ankle until you can get the victim to a hospital emergency room for treatment.

Kneecap

- Do not manipulate the injured leg. You can recognize the injury by the victim's inability to straighten the leg.
- Splint the entire leg from heel to buttocks with a board at least four inches wide; cushion the board so the leg can rest comfortably.
- Support the ankle and knee area with extra padding.
- Hold the splint in place by tying it firmly but not tightly around the leg at the ankle, above and below the knee and around the thigh.

Thigh

- Gently straighten the injured leg.
- Place a folded blanket or other soft, thick material (a folded coat, jacket, etc.) between the victim's legs.
  - Tie the two legs together in several places, avoiding the immediate area of the fracture.

Lower Leg

Follow the same procedure as for a broken thigh, above. Or, if a pillow is available, use it to cushion and immobilize the leg:

- Slide the pillow under the leg.
- Fold the ends of the pillow together and fasten with a pin or hold in place with belts, rope or whatever comparable items are available. Tie tight enough to hold the pillow in place; avoid pressure on the leg.
- For more support, place boards or sticks outside the pillow before tying.

Elbow

If the elbow is bent, *don't* try to straighten it:

- Put the victim's forearm in a sling.
- If possible, immobilize the upper arm by wrapping the entire arm, sling and all, in a towel or cloth and fastening it under the opposite arm.

If the elbow is straight:

- Immobilize the entire arm by cushioning it from the armpit to below the elbow. Tie the cushion in place without exerting pressure on the elbow.

- If boards or objects that can serve as splits are available, wrap a towel or other material around them as padding and tie around the arm above and below the injured elbow.

Hand

- Pad a splint and tie in place under the injured hand and arm.
- Bend the victim's arm at the elbow and put the lower arm into a sling (see Bandaging, above).

Collarbone

Using a piece of cloth or a large towel make a wide sling that holds the arm close to the body and keeps the upper body still. Follow the instructions and diagram on pages 9–11.

Pelvis

- With the victim lying on his back, tie the legs together. They may be straight or bent, whichever is most comfortable.
- Get medical help to move the victim. If none is available, gently slide a padded board large enough to support the entire body under the victim. Try to keep the injured person as still as possible while you do this. Make sure you do not twist or turn the body.

Broken Bones that Protrude Through the Skin

First aid is the same as for fractured bones that do not protrude through the skin. However, first you must try to stop the bleeding:

- Apply a clean pad or cloth (a sterile pad is preferred if available) to the wound and press gently.
- Do *not* try to push the broken bone back into place.
- Do *not* wash the wound or apply any medication.
- Cover the entire wound with a clean bandage and immobilize and/or splint the broken bone as described above.

CHEST PAIN

Any number of conditions, everything from indigestion to a heart attack, can cause chest pain. *Unexplained chest pain that lasts for more than two minutes should never be ignored even if the patient minimizes the discomfort. People suffering heart attacks usually deny that anything serious could be wrong.* They may attribute the discomfort to indigestion or protest that they don't want to bother the doctor or would feel foolish if their pain is a false alarm.

The signs of heart attack* include:

- A feeling of pressure, squeezing, fullness, tightness or pain in the chest.

---

* For further information on heart attacks, see Dranov, Paula. *Heart Disease: A Random House Personal Medical Handbook.* New York: Random House, 1990.

- Discomfort, usually in the center of the chest behind the breastbone. It can, however, spread to either shoulder, the neck, lower jaw or either arm.
- Pain that typically lasts longer than two minutes but can subside and then recur.

(Sharp, stabbing pains that last less than ten seconds *usually* are *not* signs of a heart attack.)

Any or all of the following symptoms may also occur:
- Sweating
- Nausea
- Shortness of breath
- Weakness

If you suspect that someone is having a heart attack, get medical help immediately.

If the victim loses consciousness, perform mouth-to-mouth resuscitation and/or cardiopulmonary resuscitation (CPR) (see pages xxxv–xxxvi).

Angina
(Angina Pectoris)

Chest pain that develops during physical exercise may be angina, a symptom of reduced blood flow to the heart. It has been described as a squeezing, choking or constricting sensation in the center of the chest that may spread to the throat, neck, jaw, teeth and cheeks.

Other symptoms include:
- Sweating
- Nausea
- Dizziness
- Breathing difficulties

People with angina should always carry medication to relieve it. Traveling companions should know where to find this medication and how to administer it.

If you suspect that chest pain is due to angina, stop moving and rest. Lie down if possible.

Administer the medication. Directions should be on the container. If they are not and the patient doesn't seem to know what to do, look for a copy of the prescription and directions for its use on pages xvii, xxi, or xxv. Some of these drugs can be administered about three times in ten minutes. This should be noted on the directions for use.

With rest and medication, angina should subside within ten minutes.

If it does not, get medical help immediately.

CHOKING

Someone who is choking usually signals distress by gasping for breath and, often, grabbing the throat. If the victim can breathe and speak, don't interfere with attempts to cough up the food or other foreign object that is responsible for the choking. If he or she cannot breathe and speak, administer the *Heimlich maneuver*:

- Stand behind the victim and place your fist with the thumb side against the stomach above the navel and below the ribs.
- Holding your fist with your other hand, thrust upward forcefully four times.
- If the victim doesn't expel the object, repeat the thrusts. Continue with the repetitions ten times.

- If the victim is lying down, straddle his or her trunk. Keeping your arms straight, place one fist thumb side down in the position described above; place your other hand on top and thrust upward four times.
- If the victim is unconscious, stretch him or her out on the floor and tilt the head backward.
- Check the victim's mouth for false teeth, chewing gum or other objects. Then pinch the nostrils closed and place your mouth over the victim's. Create a tight seal so no air escapes. Breathe forcefully into the victim's mouth four times in succession. Repeat every four to five seconds.
- If breathing does not resume, perform the Heimlich maneuver as described above for victims who are lying down.
- If this doesn't help, open the victim's mouth and sweep your fingers along the sides of the cheeks and back to the base of the tongue, checking for foreign material. If you find something you can grasp, pull it out. Be careful not to push it farther down the throat. If you can't pull it out with your fingers, do *not* try to remove it with any type of instrument.

To perform the Heimlich maneuver on a small child or infant, place the youngster on the ground and thrust as described above but with less force than you would use with an adult. As an alternative, drape the child's body over your forearm on your thigh, use the heel of your other hand to pound the back between the shoulders four times in quick succession. Use less force than you would for an adult.

CONVULSIONS

Convulsions (violent contractions of the arms, legs, body and head) can occur as a result of many different injuries or illnesses, including high fever. They may be preceded by fainting and hyperventilation.

- Protect the victim from injury by supporting the body as he or she falls.
- If necessary, move the victim away from danger (fire, stairs, etc.) and move any object that could cause injury if it is struck during the seizures.
- If possible, to prevent choking turn the victim on the side or turn the head so that saliva, vomit or mucus can drain from the mouth. Check that there is nothing (gum, food, etc.) in the mouth. You may not be able to do this if the jaw is tightly closed.
- Loosen any tight clothing around the neck and waist.
- Do *not* force anything between the teeth to stop the victim from biting or swallowing the tongue; the danger of either occurring is small.
- Shield the victim from onlookers to prevent embarrassment when he or she recovers.
- When the victim regains consciousness, encourage him or her to rest; once conscious, the victim may drink water or another clear, cool nonalcoholic beverage.
- Stay with the victim until he or she is completely recovered since patients are frequently confused and lethargic after a seizure.

- If an injury preceded the convulsions, complete first aid. Get medical assistance as soon as possible. (Also see Epilepsy, page 43.)

EYE INJURIES

Never attempt to remove anything sticking into the eyeball. Instead, gently cover *both* eyes with a clean cloth and get medical help. Any cuts to the eye or eyelid should be treated in the same manner.

To remove eyelashes or specks of dirt floating in the eye:

- Don't let the victim rub the affected eye.
- Make sure your hands are clean.
- Pull the upper eyelid down and over the lower lid and hold it in place; tearing may flood the particle out.
- If that doesn't work, rinse the eye with warm water.
- If the object doesn't rinse out and you can see it, moisten the tip of a clean cloth or tissue and lift it out.
- If you can't see anything in the eye, the ash or dirt may be on the inside of the upper lid. Ask the victim to look down and gently pull the upper lid down by the lashes. Then, place a match stick or similarly shaped clean object horizontally across the eye and gently roll the lid up so you can see the underside. Remove the speck with the moistened tip of a tissue or handkerchief.

- If you can't find the speck or lash and discomfort persists, cover the affected eye and get medical attention.
- If a chemical has splashed in the eye, immediately wash copiously with water. Get medical attention as soon as possible.

FAINTING

The most common causes of fainting are emotional shock, standing for too long in one position or heat exhaustion (see page 67). Most people recover within a few minutes. When someone feels faint, the following steps can prevent loss of consciousness:
- The victim should lie down with legs elevated about a foot above the body. As an alternative, sitting down, bending forward and placing the head between the knees may help.

When someone does faint:
- Keep the victim lying down with feet elevated.
- Loosen the collar and other tight clothing.
- Bathe the victim's face with cool water. (Don't splash water on the face.)
- If the victim fell, check to make sure no injury has occurred.
- Should the victim vomit, turn the head to the side to prevent choking.
- Make sure the victim is breathing normally; if he or she is not, maintain an open airway by making sure nothing is obstructing the throat.

• Don't offer any food or drink until you are sure the victim is completely recovered.

HEAD, NECK AND BACK INJURIES

Because head, neck and back injuries can lead to permanent paralysis and/or death, you must summon medical help at once. Send someone for medical help or go yourself if the victim is in no danger of further injury and does not require cardiopulmonary resuscitation or mouth-to-mouth resuscitation. Do not leave the victim alone for more than a minute.

• Do *not* move the victim unless absolutely necessary (danger of fire, explosion, drowning).
• If you must move the victim, slide a board under the body; it should be wide enough to support the entire torso and long enough to reach from buttocks to head. Do this slowly and gently so that the victim's body remains as still as possible.
• Before moving the board, tie the victim to it by wrapping strips of cloth around the board and across the forehead, under the armpits and around the lower abdomen.
• If the victim is lying facedown, get help so that the entire body can be turned at once without twisting or moving any area.
• If the victim is unconscious, you may have to administer mouth-to-mouth resuscitation and if you cannot detect a pulse, you will have to administer cardiopulmonary resuscitation. These techniques appear on pages xxxv–xxxvi.

- If the victim is conscious, do not let him or her move.
- If you can't get medical help and must take the victim to the hospital yourself, slide him or her onto a cushioned board or other support without changing the position in which he or she fell or was found. Make sure the head remains still. Tie the board to the victim as described above.

Cuts on the Head

If the injury appears limited to cuts on the scalp, try to stop the bleeding with gentle pressure. Even relatively minor scalp injuries can bleed profusely.

- Clean minor cuts with soap and water and then apply a sterile bandage.
- Do *not* try to clean severe cuts; instead, apply a sterile bandage and press gently but firmly to stop the bleeding.

Possible Skull Fractures

If the victim is unconscious and not breathing, perform mouth-to-mouth resuscitation (see page xxxvi). Assume that anyone found unconscious has a head injury and may also have a neck injury.

If the victim is conscious and has pain in the back or neck or cannot move his arms, hands, fingers, legs, feet and toes, *do not move him*. However, if the victim is in danger of further injury and must be moved without medical assistance:

- Follow the procedure outlined above under back injuries on page 21 and place pillows or folded coats on either side of the head to prevent it from turning.

With all head injuries, watch for the following symptoms of brain injury:

- Drowsiness, confusion, difficulty speaking
- Bleeding or a clear liquid flowing from the nose, ear or mouth
- Pallor *or* a flushed face
- Headache
- Vomiting
- One pupil in the eyes larger than the other
- Restlessness
- Convulsions

If the victim is unconscious:

- Make sure that he or she is breathing and has a clear airway—check to make sure that the tongue is not blocking the throat.

If there is no sign of a neck injury and the victim is conscious:

- Gently raise the head slightly and turn it away from the injured area of the head to relieve pressure.

In either case, get medical help and keep the victim warm and comfortable until help arrives.

- *Never* give the victim anything to eat or drink and do *not* administer any drugs.

Neck Injuries

Neck injuries and head injuries frequently go together. Because of the possibility of paralysis, people with neck injuries should *never* be moved by anyone other than medical personnel except when there is immediate danger of further injury.

Always suspect neck injury when the victim cannot move or cannot move the arms or legs or feels a tingling sensation in the hands or feet.

Other indications of neck injury include head injury, headache, stiff neck.

While waiting for medical help:
- Keep the victim warm.
- Keep the head and neck still with pillows, towels or clothing. Hold these in place with heavy objects that can't be easily pushed aside.

If you must move the victim:
- Cushion the neck and head with towels or clothing to prevent movement or twisting. Make sure the victim can breathe easily.
- Get help (you'll need three people) to slide a heavy board big enough to hold the entire body under the victim.
1. Be very careful not to twist the victim's body in the process. It should be kept still and in the same position.
2. One person should hold the head and neck still while the others lift the body just enough to allow the board to be slipped underneath. This should be done *in one motion*. If the victim was not found lying faceup, you will have to turn him as you place him on the board.
3. Tie the victim to the board if possible to prevent movement in transport.

Broken Back

The procedure for assisting someone with a broken back is the same as for a broken neck or neck injury (see above) except that victims usually are found lying facedown and must be transported to the hospital *in the same position*.

HYPERVENTILATION
(ANXIETY ATTACK)

Some people react to tension and emotional upsets by breathing more rapidly than normal. They may become light-headed and complain of tingling and numbness in the hands, feet and around the mouth. Hyperventilation can lower levels of carbon dioxide in the blood, leading to muscle tightness in the throat and chest that can be mistaken for a heart attack. Occasionally, hyperventilation can result in convulsions.

Hyperventilation can usually be brought under control by having the victim breathe into a paper bag for a few minutes. Make sure the bag covers the nose and mouth. The paper-bag technique forces the victim to rebreathe air and carbon dioxide, which restores normal breathing.

If hyperventilation persists despite the paper-bag treatment, get medical help.

NOSEBLEEDS

Press your thumbs against the upper lip just below the nose.

If that doesn't stem the flow:

- Insert a small wad of sterile absorbent cotton into each nostril. Make sure that some protrudes so that the packing can be pulled out easily when bleeding subsides.
- With the cotton in place, pinch the nostrils together and maintain the pressure for *exactly* six minutes. If bleeding doesn't subside, get medical help.

SHOCK

Shock is a drop in blood pressure accompanied by other internal changes that can cause death, even when the precipitating injury is not life-threatening. *To be safe, assume that shock will occur after any serious injury.* Symptoms include:

- Pale, moist and clammy skin; there may be a bluish tinge
- Weakness
- A rapid, weak pulse
- Shallow, irregular breathing; frequent sighing
- Thirst
- Vomiting
- Dull and sunken eyes; dilated pupils
- Unconsciousness

Follow the precautions listed below after any serious injury whether or not signs of shock are apparent:

- Summon medical help.
- Keep the victim lying down.
- Make sure the airway is open.
- Appropriately treat the injury.
- Keep the victim warm but not overheated; you may have to place a blanket under someone who is lying on the ground or floor.
- Check for injuries that might not be obvious, and administer first aid for any you find.
- Unless there is abdominal pain or a head or neck injury, give the victim something salty to drink, and later something sweet. However, *do not* give coffee, alcohol or any other stimulant.
- If you were not present when the accident occurred, get as much information as possible about what happened; this can help doctors should the victim be unable to talk to them.

UNCONSCIOUSNESS

Any number of injuries or health problems can lead to unconsciousness. If the victim is breathing, take the following steps:

- If you know what led to the unconsciousness and are *sure* that the victim has no head or neck injury and no broken bones, turn him on his side. This will help maintain an open airway and allow mucus to drain from the nose and/or mouth. The head should be slightly lower than the rest of the body.

- If the victim has had an accident and you suspect a head or neck injury, keep the head still but elevate the chin and make sure there is nothing in the mouth to obstruct breathing.
- Provide first aid for any obvious and serious injuries that may have led to the unconsciousness.
- Keep the victim comfortably warm; do *not* attempt to give him anything to drink or eat.
- Do *not* leave the victim alone.
- Get medical help.
- If the victim is not breathing, perform mouth-to-mouth resuscitation or cardiopulmonary resuscitation (pages xxxv–xxxvi).

PART II

SPECIAL NEEDS

▼

NOTE

If you have a health problem that could lead to an emergency when you are away from home, place a paper clip or other marker on the relevant page so you can turn to it quickly should first aid be needed.

If you are the patient, you may be able to cope alone or you may need help. Ask your spouse, parent or other close relative, traveling companion, teacher or coach to read and become familiar with the instructions that pertain to your condition.

Anyone with an allergy, asthma, epilepsy, diabetes or other chronic condition should wear a MedicAlert tag or bracelet so that emergency medical personnel will know how to proceed should help be needed. To order MedicAlert identification, telephone 1 (800) ID-ALERT. You should also carry a card in your wallet noting any ongoing health problem.

INDEX

ANAPHYLAXIS

THIS is a life-threatening emergency that can affect people who are allergic* to insect stings, certain foods or drugs. Anyone susceptible to these attacks should carry an emergency kit containing injectable epinephrine to bring symptoms under control.

Symptoms include:
- Red, itchy rash
- Hives
- Flushed face
- Feeling of apprehension
- Palpitations
- Fainting
- Feeling uncomfortably hot
- Dizziness
- Nausea, vomiting, diarrhea, abdominal cramps
- Shortness of breath

---

* For further information on allergies, see Dranov, Paula. *Allergies: A Random House Personal Medical Handbook*. New York: Random House, 1990.

- Tightness in the chest
- Wheezing
- Loss of consciousness

Anaphylaxis requires immediate action. There are two alternatives:

- Administer injectable epinephrine.
- Get immediate medical help.

If epinephrine is available, you must inject it as soon as possible after the onset of symptoms. There are two types of injectable epinephrine on the market, EpiPen and the AnaKit.

EpiPen is an automatic injector. Directions for use:

- Pull off the gray safety cap.
- Place the black tip on the outer thigh.
- Push the EpiPen against the skin and hold in place for several seconds. It will automatically inject a premeasured dose of epinephrine.

AnaKit provides a syringe with a preloaded, measured dose of epinephrine. Directions for use:

- Remove the protective sheath from the syringe.
- Inject the epinephrine into the outer thigh or upper arm.
- After administering epinephrine, take the patient to the hospital. Further treatment may be needed to prevent a recurrence.

Additional Precautions:

- Get a new supply of epinephrine after using the one you have.
- Periodically check the expiration date on your epi-

nephrine emergency kit to be sure it will be effective should you need it.
- Always have one kit at home and one in the car.

ASTHMA ATTACKS

One or more of the following symptoms may occur:
- Tightness in the chest
- Shortness of breath
- Coughing
- Wheezing
- Anxiety
- Coughing up thick mucus

Less common symptoms include rapid heartbeat, restlessness, pallor, fatigue, vomiting and postnasal drip.

Attacks can develop suddenly, but most victims learn to recognize early warning signs that can occur as much as a day in advance. Breathing changes are the most common warnings, although a wide range of physical symptoms and mood or behavioral changes are possible. Parents of asthmatic children should be able to recognize the complaints, breathing and behavior changes that signal an approaching attack. Among them:
- Coughing
- Shortness of breath
- Tightness in the chest
- Breathing through the mouth
- Increased pulse rate

- Fatigue
- Itching at the back of the throat
- Not feeling well
- Nervousness
- Irritability
- Tendency to become easily upset

Affected children can become overactive or else unusually quiet. Less common signs of an impending attack include perspiration, pallor (or a reddened face), swelling in the face, dark circles under the eyes, flared nostrils.

Once early warning signs appear, the patient can take the following steps to head off or reduce the attack's severity:

- Stop what you are doing and relax. If you are among the asthmatics who do breathing exercises to help manage attacks, begin them now.
- Drink liquids. They replace fluids in the airways that evaporate as breathing changes. The fluids also thin and help expel mucus that forms during an attack. Warm liquids can help relax the airways. Tea, coffee, clear soup, warm cider, are all appropriate. If warm liquids aren't available, cold ones will do. Drink as much as possible, at least eight ounces every half hour.
- Administer medication. Asthmatics usually carry a bronchodilator to relieve symptoms. Some of these drugs can be taken by mouth, but most must be inhaled.

Severe Asthma Attacks

Attacks that continue or worsen despite treatment are known as *status asthmaticus* and require medical attention. The following symptoms indicate that an emergency is developing:

- Labored breathing
- Breathing from the neck up
- Perspiration
- Flared nostrils
- Raised shoulders
- Indentation at hollow of the neck
- Fearfulness
- Holding hands over the head
- Lips and fingernail beds turn blue. *This is an indication of cyanosis, a lack of oxygen.*

Should any or all of these symptoms develop, take the patient to the nearest hospital emergency room immediately.

Exercise-Induced Asthma

Up to 90 percent of all people with asthma are susceptible to attacks brought on by exercise.

These episodes usually occur after, not during, exercise. Most are brief and subside within minutes, but some can continue for up to two hours or persist and progress into status asthmaticus. Although most attacks begin five to ten minutes after exercise, some delayed reactions develop four to ten hours later.

Symptoms range from coughing to tightness in the chest, wheezing and shortness of breath. Children may complain of stomach cramps, and some people develop headaches that probably are related to an underlying sinus condition or nasal congestion.

As a rule, attacks occur only when exercise is strenuous enough to raise an adult's heart rate to 150 beats per minute and a child's to 170. Running, jogging and cold-weather sports such as ice hockey and skiing are most likely to provoke an attack.

Anyone susceptible to exercise-induced asthma should avoid or cut back on exercise under the following conditions:

- Bad air pollution (sulfur-dioxide levels of 0.5 parts per million; ozone levels of 0.9 parts per million)
- Very cold weather (temperatures significantly lower than those you are accustomed to)
- A high pollen count
- A respiratory-tract infection

A few minutes' rest should bring symptoms under control; if it does not, two inhalations of a bronchodilator usually works. Otherwise, consult Severe Asthma Attacks, page 35.

DIABETES

Hypoglycemia/Insulin Reaction

This usually occurs among diabetics* who take insulin, but it can affect those on oral diabetic drugs.

---

* For further information on diabetes, see Dranov, Paula. *Diabetes: A Random House Personal Medical Handbook.* New York: Random House, 1990.

Hypoglycemia (low blood sugar) can occur when a diabetic has not eaten on schedule, has been exercising without eating something first, or has been drinking alcohol on an empty stomach. Taking too much insulin or too large a dose of an oral drug to control blood sugar can also be responsible. Initial symptoms include shakiness, light-headedness, irritability, nervousness, confusion, pounding heart, numbness or tingling in lips or tongue, hunger.

If not treated, the reaction can proceed to a second stage characterized by drowsiness, headache, blurry vision, nausea, lack of coordination, confused conversation, mood changes.

A third, "crisis," stage brings on seizures, unconsciousness, coma.

Treatment

Act quickly. Give the victim something sweet to eat or drink—a candy bar, fruit juice or a soft drink (regular, *not* no-cal)—to bring blood sugar up and end the reaction. Diabetics taking insulin should be carrying an appropriate sweet snack, glucose tablets or gel.

Act quickly. An unconscious victim *must* have an injection of glucagon immediately. Family, friends, teachers, traveling companions, etc., should know where to find and how to use the patient's glucagon supplies or emergency kit. Here are step-by-step directions:

- Check to be sure the expiration date hasn't passed.
- If more than one person is present, have someone call the doctor (see pages xv, xix, xxiii for the tele-

phone number) or summon emergency medical help (dial 911 in most areas of the United States or ask the operator for the local emergency number).

- Turn the patient on his or her side or face down.
- If there are two bottles, unseal both and clean the tops with alcohol. (Some kits have only one bottle, containing powdered glucagon, and a syringe containing a diluting solution.)
- If there are two bottles, one (usually labeled #1) contains a diluting solution; the other (labeled #2) contains the powdered glucagon. Pull off the shield and draw the diluting liquid into the syringe. Inject it into the vial of glucagon.
- Shake the combined contents of the vial.
- Withdraw the entire contents into the syringe.
- If using a kit with a syringe containing the diluting solution, pull off the shield and inject the contents of the syringe into the vial of glucagon. Shake until mixed, and withdraw the contents into the syringe.
- Pinch a fold of skin in the patient's arm, buttocks, thigh or abdomen, and inject all the glucagon.
- Withdraw the needle, and clean the injection site with alcohol.
- If there was no one available to call for help earlier, make the phone call now.
- Get something sweet for the patient to eat when he or she regains consciousness, and have another snack—a sandwich or some crackers—ready. Eating will prevent a second episode.

If the patient doesn't awaken within twenty minutes, administer more glucagon. There is no danger of an overdose.

Diabetic Coma

The following symptoms indicate that internal changes are taking place that can result in a diabetic coma:

- Increased thirst
- Frequent urination
- Sudden weight loss
- Nausea and vomiting
- Stomach pains
- Dry, flushed skin
- Drowsiness
- Difficulty breathing
- Fruity-smelling breath

If unchecked (consult a doctor to adjust insulin dosage), a diabetic coma can ensue. The process leading up to the coma can take days.

There is no first aid for a diabetic coma. Get the patient to an emergency room as soon as possible. Tell the admitting nurse you suspect the patient may be in a diabetic coma.

Treatment in the hospital will include insulin to reduce blood sugar, and fluids because the patient may be dehydrated from vomiting and/or urinating.

Hyperosmolar Coma
(Nonketotic Hyperglycemic
Hyperosmolar Coma)

This potentially life-threatening condition usually affects older people with diabetes. (In undiagnosed cases, it may be the first diabetes symptom.) It is usually triggered by illness, infection, emotional stress, certain drugs (steroids, diuretics, tranquilizers).

Symptoms leading to hyperosmolar coma include:
- Weakness, fatigue
- Extreme thirst
- Dehydration
- Dry mouth
- Shallow breathing
- Flushed, dry skin
- Mental confusion
- Drowsiness
- Stupor

There is no first aid.

Get the patient to the nearest hospital. If you are not far from the patient's home, see pages xv, xix, or xxiii for the address or ambulance or emergency telephone number. Notify the patient's doctor (name and telephone number are listed on pages xv, xix, or xxiii).

Treatment includes insulin and fluids.

DRUG OVERDOSE

Anyone who takes drugs as treatment for a health problem or recreationally could inadvertently overdose. Symptoms and treatment for overdose with drugs prescribed or recommended by a doctor for a specific medical condition should be entered in the drug diary for the affected member of the family. Here's a rundown on the symptoms of and first aid for overdose of alcohol, illicit drugs and commonly prescribed tranquilizers and stimulants:

Alcohol

Symptoms of overdose:
- Intoxication (slurred speech, lack of coordination)
- Vomiting
- Abnormal breathing
- Unconsciousness

A victim who is asleep and can be easily roused requires no treatment. For abnormal breathing or unconsciousness, restore breathing and circulation via mouth-to-mouth resuscitation or CPR (pages xxxv–xxxvi) and get medical help.

Stimulants

These include amphetamines ("speed") including benzedrine, dexedrine and methedrine as well as the illicit drugs cocaine and its derivative "crack."

Overdose symptoms include hyperactive behavior, aggression, confusion, irritability, fear, suspiciousness, repeatedly performing the same act, an unrealistic or exaggerated sense of capability.

As drug effects wear off, the drug abuser may fall into a deep sleep or suffer hallucinations. Depression, dehydration and voracious hunger can also occur.

Try to prevent the person from harming others or endangering him or herself. Maintain an open airway if the victim is in deep sleep. You may have to perform mouth-to-mouth resuscitation or CPR (pages xxxv–xxxvi).

Get medical help.

Barbiturates and Narcotics

The most widely used barbiturates are Nembutol, Seconal, codeine and phenobarbital. Prescribed for a wide variety of medical conditions, they are physically addicting and must be withdrawn gradually to prevent symptoms including cramps, nausea, convulsions and, rarely, sudden death.

Withdrawal from the following illicit drugs causes similar symptoms: heroin, opium, morphine, synthetic heroin (Fentanyl), marijuana and hashish.

Symptoms of overdose are similar to those of alcohol intoxication: confusion, slurred speech, disorientation, lack of physical coordination, an inability to concentrate, aggression and, eventually, deep sleep.

- A drug user who falls asleep but can be roused should be forced to walk until the drug effects wear off.
- Get medical attention for anyone who can't be roused.
- If the victim is not breathing, you may have to perform mouth-to-mouth resuscitation (page xxxvi) until medical help arrives.

Tranquilizers

Halcion, Valium and Xanax are among the most commonly prescribed tranquilizers. Symptoms of overdose include drowsiness, weakness, a feeling of drunkenness, a lack of coordination, tremor and stupor leading to deep sleep. An overdose is unlikely to be fatal except when combined with alcohol and/or barbiturates.

- Get medical attention for anyone who has taken an overdose.

Hallucinogens

These include LSD, PCP, mescaline, psilocybin (mushrooms).

Overdose symptoms include delusions, hallucinations, enlarged pupils, facial redness, inappropriate emotional responses including uncontrollable laughing and/or crying, depression, panic, fear, tension, disorientation.

- Try to keep the victim calm in quiet and safe surroundings where neither the victim nor others can be injured.
- Don't startle the victim by making sudden moves.
- Get medical attention.

EPILEPSY

People with epilepsy often have some warning (aura) that a seizure is imminent. However, in many cases, the first sign that a seizure (convulsions) is beginning is a short, involuntary cry or scream. The victim will twitch, may stop breathing temporarily, may vomit and/or lose control of his or her bladder or bowels. The face and lips may turn blue, and the eyes may roll upward.

Not much needs to be done during a seizure:

- If the victim starts to fall, support his or her body and lay it down gently.
- If necessary, move the victim away from danger

(stairs, a fire, etc.) and move any objects that could cause injury if the victim's body strikes them during the seizure.

- Don't interfere with the convulsion or hold the victim down.
- Do *not* try to force anything between the teeth to prevent the victim from biting or swallowing the tongue; the danger of either occurring is small, and you could cause an injury.
- Do *not* throw water on the victim.
- Loosen any tight clothing around the neck and waist.
- If possible, turn the victim on the side or turn the head so that saliva, vomit or mucus can drain from the mouth. (This may not be possible if the jaw is tightly clenched.)
- Shield the victim from onlookers to prevent embarrassment when he or she recovers.
- When the victim regains consciousness, encourage him or her to rest; once fully conscious, the victim may drink water or any other clear, nonalcoholic beverage. Stay with the victim until he or she is fully recovered. There may be some lethargy or confusion in the aftermath of a seizure.
- Seek medical attention for seizures that continue for longer than five minutes or when a series of seizures occur.

Convulsions also can occur as a result of a high fever, head injury, poisoning, electric shock, drug withdrawal, insect or snake bites. First aid is the same as for epileptic seizures, but get immediate medical attention afterward for the injury that precipitated the seizure.

PREGNANCY

Any abdominal pain, cramping or vaginal bleeding during pregnancy could indicate miscarriage and requires immediate medical attention. Other symptoms that may mean trouble and should be promptly evaluated by a doctor include persistent vomiting, severe headaches, swollen face or fingers, vision disturbances (blurring, dimness), chills, fever, sudden leaking of fluid from the vagina. Do not attempt to treat any of these symptoms before consulting a physician.

Ectopic Pregnancy

This occurs when the fertilized egg is embedded in a fallopian tube instead of the uterus. In some instances, a woman doesn't even realize that she is pregnant. An ectopic pregnancy is a dangerous, life-threatening condition that will require surgery. Symptoms include spotting of blood from the vagina, cramps or sudden, severe abdominal pain, vomiting and, occasionally, prostration. This is an emergency requiring immediate medical attention. If possible, call the woman's doctor for instructions. If not, take her to the nearest hospital. Do *not* give her anything to eat or drink (not even water). She will require immediate surgery.

Emergency Childbirth

When you are far from the hospital or the midwife or physician who was supposed to deliver the baby and an expectant mother announces that childbirth is imminent, try to summon medical help. While you wait, prepare for delivery by boiling water to sterilize scissors or a knife (leave them in the boiling water for at least five minutes). An alternative is to hold the scissors or knife over a flame for at least thirty seconds. You will also need clean cloths, towels or clothing to place under the mother during delivery and others to wrap the newborn afterward.

Childbirth can progress very quickly. Here's a step-by-step guide to delivering the baby:

- Have the mother lie down on her back, her knees bent and her thighs widely separated.
- Don't touch her vagina or the baby's head once it appears.
- Once the head is out of the vagina, support it gently. The rest of the body should follow quickly, but you may have to lower the baby's head slightly to allow the upper shoulder to emerge and then raise it so the lower shoulder can slip out. Work gently.
- If the umbilical cord is wrapped around the baby's neck, slip it over the head. If it is tightly wrapped (an unlikely event) tie off the cord as described below and cut with the sterilized knife or scissors.
- The baby's body will be *very slippery*, so handle with care.
- The baby should cry loudly once it is out of the

mother's body. If it does not, hold it firmly by the ankles and tap gently on the upper back. If the baby still doesn't cry and isn't breathing, perform mouth-to-mouth resuscitation (page xxxvi) covering both the infant's mouth *and* nose with your mouth.

- Wipe the baby's mouth and nose to make sure nothing interferes with breathing, but do not clean the eyes or ears or remove the protective coating covering the skin.
- Place the baby on the mother's abdomen. It isn't necessary to cut the umbilical cord if you can take the mother to the hospital now. If you can't, once the cord stops pulsing, tie a clean strip of cloth around it about four inches from the baby's body and another strip two inches farther along toward the mother's body. The knots should be tight enough to prevent bleeding from either end once the cord is cut. Cut the cord between the two ties with the sterilized scissors or knife. Wrap the baby in a clean towel, blanket or cloth. Make sure the head (not the face) is covered and place the baby next to the mother with the head slightly lower than the rest of the body.
- The afterbirth will occur within ten to twenty minutes. Catch it in a plastic bag and save it for medical examination later. (A doctor or midwife can determine whether the entire afterbirth was delivered.)
- Place sanitary napkins or a clean cloth over the vagina to absorb remaining blood.
- Place hand on the woman's abdomen below the navel. You will feel the uterus, which is the size

and shape of a large ball. Massage the uterus every five minutes for an hour or until medical help arrives to control bleeding.

- Keep the mother warm and comfortable. Sponge off her face. She can have tea, coffee, water or clear broth. Do *not* give her any alcoholic beverage or aspirin. Either may increase her bleeding. If she has bled a great deal, elevate her feet to prevent shock.
- Get medical attention for both mother and baby.

PART III

IN THE CAR

▼

INDEX

FIRST-AID KIT

Flashlight
Bandages, assorted
Roll sterile gauze bandage
Dozen gauze pads (4" x 4")
Butterfly bandages
Elastic bandage (3" wide)
Adhesive tape (waterproof)
Absorbent cotton
Scissors
Tweezers
Sewing needle (for removing splinters)
Safety pins (large)
Aspirin
Acetominophen (if traveling with children)
Calamine lotion
Ipecac (to induce vomiting)
Antihistamine
Hydrogen peroxide
Insect repellent
Insect spray

Plain or antiseptic soap (one bar)
Rubbing alcohol

BLACK EYES

These common injuries stem from blows. Symptoms include pain and reddened skin that later turns black and blue and eventually fades to yellow. Sometimes a lump develops at the point of injury.

Treat first with frequent applications of cold compresses or ice. After forty-eight hours, switch to moist heat (a warm, wet washcloth or other compress).

Seek medical treatment for black eyes that are very painful, if there is severe swelling or if there are any vision problems.

BRUISES

Most bruises in the car are caused by blows upon impact. Symptoms include pain, reddened skin that later turns black and blue and eventually fades to yellow. There may be some swelling.

- Treat first with cold compresses or ice frequently applied.
- After forty-eight hours, switch to moist heat (a warm, wet washcloth or other compress).
- Seek medical attention for bruises that are very painful and accompanied by severe swelling.

BURNS

Burns can result from automobile accidents involving fire, from accidentally touching hot metal when attempting repairs under the hood or from overheated radiators.

First-Degree Burns

These commonly result from touching hot objects or exposure to steam. Symptoms include redness, pain and, sometimes, swelling. Skin is unbroken. No blisters appear.

The burned area should be placed under cold running water as soon as possible or covered with a cold wet compress. If water is not available, use any cold liquid.

Cover the burn with a bandage or clean cloth. Don't apply ointments, grease or butter. A doctor may recommend an antiseptic ointment if the burn remains painful.

Second-Degree Burns

These more extensive injuries can cause damage below the surface of the skin. Symptoms include blisters or oozing, pain, redness and swelling.

- Immediately treat with cold water or use any cold liquid (including soft drinks, milk, beer).
- Continue to pour cold liquids on the burn until the pain diminishes.

- Pat the area dry and cover with a clean cloth.
- Get medical help. The more widespread the burn, the more urgent the need for prompt medical attention.

Third-Degree Burns

These are the most severe type of burns. All layers of skin are affected and there may be some charring. If you suspect a third-degree burn, summon medical help immediately. First-aid measures include:

- Smother the flames if the victim is on fire. Any heavy cloth will do.
- Treat the victim for shock: Keep the victim lying down; elevate the feet unless he or she is unconscious or has neck, back, head, chest or other severe injuries.
- Don't remove any clothes stuck to the burn or attempt to clean the burned area.
- Don't put cold water or ice on the burns.
- Don't apply any ointments or other burn remedies.
- If the burns are on the face or neck, prop up the back and make sure, if he or she is having difficulty breathing, that the airways are clear.

CARBON-MONOXIDE POISONING

Sitting in a closed car with the motor running or even riding in a car with the windows closed can lead to carbon-monoxide poisoning if this by-product of combustion isn't properly vented. Symptoms are headache, yawning, dizziness, faintness, ringing in the ears, nausea, bright red skin, overwhelming lethargy, stupor and coma.

- Get the victim out of the car into fresh air immediately.
- Perform mouth-to-mouth resuscitation or CPR (pages xxxv–xxxvi) if the victim is not breathing and/or a heartbeat or pulse cannot be detected.
- Get medical help. Further treatment will be required to rid the body of the effects of carbon-monoxide poisoning.

FINGERTIP INJURIES

Slamming a car door on the fingers can result in severe bruising. Initial symptoms are, of course, pain, reddened skin that later turns black and blue and then fades to yellow.

- Frequently apply ice or cold compresses.
- After forty-eight hours, switch to warm, wet compresses.
- Seek medical attention for severe pain and swelling and to drain the dark pool of blood that forms under the nail of an injured fingertip. Drainage may prevent the nail from coming off as a result of the injury. A doctor will be able to determine whether the fingertip is broken.

INSECT STINGS

Bees or other insects sometimes get in the car. This can be very dangerous when you are driving. Pull over to the side of the road immediately and get the bee out before you resume driving. Insect stings are most threatening to people who are allergic to the venom of bees, wasps and other stinging insects. However, stings can be painful to anyone and can also cause local infection. If you are allergic to insect stings, see page 31 in the section on Special Needs.

Typical symptoms of insect stings are pain, swelling, redness, itching and/or burning. If the insect was a bee, a tiny black stinger may protrude from the skin at the site of the sting. Flick or scrape it off quickly—squeezing and lifting it out will inject more venom under the skin.

After the stinger is removed, and for all other insect stings:

- Wash the affected area with soap and water.
- Cold compresses or ice will reduce discomfort and stop the venom from spreading.
- A topical antihistamine, calamine lotion or a paste made of baking soda and water applied to the skin can be soothing.
- Multiple stings can cause a more serious, toxic reaction. Symptoms include swelling, headache, muscle cramps, fever, drowsiness, unconsciousness. They require the same care as for one sting, but you should get medical help as soon as possible. Anyone who develops hives, breathing prob-

lems or throat tightness after a bee sting requires *immediate* medical attention.

KNOCKED-OUT TOOTH

- Have the victim bite down on a piece of clean, folded cloth to stop the bleeding.
- If the victim is a small child who has lost a ''baby tooth'' there is no need to save the tooth.
- If a permanent tooth is lost, find it.
- Wrap the tooth in a cool wet cloth or put it in a container of whole milk, *not* skim milk.

Rush both victim and tooth to the nearest dentist or hospital emergency room.

SEVERED LIMB

These are horrible injuries with a great deal of blood loss. The victim may vomit, go into shock, and/or become unconscious.

- If the victim is not breathing, you will have to perform mouth-to-mouth resuscitation and/or CPR (pages xxxv–xxxvi).
- Attempt to stop the bleeding using the techniques described on page 4.
- If you are *sure* that there is no neck injury and the victim is vomiting, turn the head to the side to prevent choking.
- Summon prompt medical attention.

After you have attended to the victim, place the severed arm, leg, finger or toe in a clean plastic bag and, if possible, surround the bag (not the limb) with ice. Ideally, you should place the limb in one bag and the ice in another bag or container. You then can put the bag containing the limb in the container of ice. If you do this, there is a possibility that an expert surgical team will be able to reattach the severed limb.

WHIPLASH

Even minor automobile accidents can result in whiplash, an injury to the neck and upper part of the spine that occurs upon impact when the body is jerked forward and then thrust sharply backward. Symptoms can include a severe headache; severe, intermittent pain in the back of the neck that radiates up into the skull and down into the lower jaw, shoulders and chest. Pain and/or numbness may radiate into the arms. The victim may be stunned or dazed and may lose consciousness briefly. Symptoms may not appear for several hours after the accident.

Victims should see a physician as quickly as possible; hospitalization may be necessary, although bed rest at home is usually adequate treatment.

AT THE BEACH

▼

INDEX

FIRST-AID KIT

Sunscreen
Sunglasses
Lotion or ointment to soothe sunburned skin
Flashlight
Bandages, assorted
Roll sterile gauze bandage
Dozen gauze pads (4″ x 4″)
Butterfly bandages
Elastic bandage (3″ wide)
Adhesive tape (waterproof)
Absorbent cotton
Scissors
Thermometer
Tweezers
Sewing needle (for removing splinters)
Safety pins (large)
Aspirin
Acetominophen (if traveling with children)
Calamine lotion
Ipecac (to induce vomiting)

Antihistamine
Hydrogen peroxide
Insect repellent
Insect spray
Plain or antiseptic soap (one bar)
Rubbing alcohol
Spirits of ammonia

SAFETY PRECAUTIONS

- Apply sunscreen before arriving at the beach (it takes up to thirty minutes to reach peak effectiveness). An SPF of 15 or higher is recommended.
- Reapply sunscreen after swimming or if you towel off perspiration.
- Wear a hat.
- If the beach has no lifeguard, is remote or isolated, make a note of the nearest telephone and tell someone responsible where you will be and when you expect to return.
- Carry a supply of coins for telephoning.
- Investigate whether there are treacherous currents or a rocky bottom in the sea whenever visiting unfamiliar, unguarded beaches.
- Don't swim, boat or surf alone at an isolated beach.

THE BENDS AND BAROTRAUMA
(DECOMPRESSION SICKNESS; CAISSON DISEASE)

This condition affects divers who surface too quickly from very deep water. It is caused by air bubbles of nitrogen forming in the blood and can be fatal if one of these bubbles travels to the brain. Symptoms include pain (the victim may double over), breathing difficulties, paralysis, joint pain.

Bleeding from the nose and ears usually is related to barotrauma, a rapid expansion of compressed air upon rising from a depth.

- Maintain an open airway and, if necessary, perform mouth-to-mouth resuscitation (page xxxvi) to restore breathing; if the victim's heart isn't beating or you can't find a pulse, perform CPR (page xxxv).
- Get medical help immediately.

CHILLS

Chills can be a response to cold temperatures or cold water or may signify some type of infection or illness. Sometimes chills can be quite severe, with violent shaking of the body.

- Keep victims comfortable and warm. If possible, use several blankets.
- If the victim is not nauseated or vomiting, hot liquids including tea, coffee, hot chocolate or soup can be warming.
- Seek medical help if chills are followed by fever or other symptoms indicating that illness, not cold temperatures, caused the chills.

DEHYDRATION

Lack of water due to excessive sweating in hot weather or loss of body fluids because of diarrhea or vomiting can lead to extreme thirst, fatigue, dizziness and abdominal or muscle cramps. Dehydration can be life-threatening, particularly among infants and the elderly.

- Move the victim into a cool, shady area.
- Give fluids to drink: water, with one-half teaspoon of salt per eight ounces or clear broth. If only carbonated beverages are available, shake them to eliminate the fizz.
- Seek medical treatment for persistent symptoms or if the victim experiences nausea, diarrhea or convulsions.

DROWNING

To rescue a drowning person within reach of the shore, a pier or boat, extend a pole, an oar, rope, or other object that he or she can grasp and hold while being pulled to safety. If available, a life preserver or flotation cushion can support the victim until you are able to get close enough for rescue. Do not try to rescue someone with your arm or leg. You are likely to be pulled into the water.

- If the victim is not breathing, start mouth-to-mouth resuscitation (page xxxvi) at once, as soon as his or her head is out of the water; you will have to administer CPR (page xxxv) if you can't detect a pulse or heartbeat.

- Once the victim is breathing normally, watch him or her carefully for signs of shock (page 26).
- Keep the victim comfortably warm but do not give food or water.
- Seek medical attention immediately since there may be a delayed reaction that requires emergency measures. This applies to people who were breathing normally when rescued as well as to those who had to be resuscitated.
- If you suspect a back or neck injury due to a diving or surfboard accident, slide the victim out of the water onto a surfboard or other wide board that can fully support the body from head to buttocks. If no board is available, pull the victim out of the water by the armpits or legs in the direction of the length of the body. Avoid twisting the body or moving the head in any direction although, if the victim is rescued facedown, you will have to turn him or her over carefully to perform mouth-to-mouth resuscitation or CPR (pages xxxv–xxxvi). (Also see Shallow-Water Blackout, page 71.)

EAR INJURIES

Diving and waterskiing accidents can lead to ear injuries, and swimming in unclean water can trigger an infection called "swimmer's ear."

Symptoms of ear injury include bleeding from the ear, pain and hearing loss.

- If a head injury has occurred, treat that first according to the instructions on page 21.
- Do not try to stem the flow of blood from the ear; do not insert cotton packing or anything else.
- Cover the ear with a clean cloth or bandage to prevent blood from dripping.
- Have the victim lie down so that the injured ear is toward the ground and can drain (however, do not move anyone who has suffered a serious head, neck or back injury).
- Get medical help.

Swimmer's Ear

Symptoms include pain, itching and, sometimes, a discharge from the ear.
- See a doctor promptly; the infection causing the symptoms will require treatment with an antibiotic.
- Do not insert anything in the ear.

FISHHOOK INJURY

A common injury among fishermen, this occurs when a hook gets caught in the body.
- If the point of the hook has pierced the skin, slide it out in the direction of entry.
- If the hook is embedded, push it through the skin until the barb emerges.
- Clip off the end with the barb (use pliers or clippers) and back the other end out in the direction it entered the skin.

• Clean the wound with soap and water and see a doctor; the victim may need a tetanus shot.

HEAT CRAMPS

Heavy sweating as a result of strenuous activity can lead to heat cramps. Symptoms are muscle pain, particularly in the calves or abdomen.
• Help the victim to a cool, shaded spot.
• Massage the cramped muscle.
• As long as the victim is not vomiting, give him or her juice, soda or a flavored beverage like Gatorade.

HEAT EXHAUSTION

Heat exhaustion typically occurs among people who are not used to hot weather. It affects women more often than men and is more common among those of both sexes who tend to perspire a lot.

Symptoms include heavy sweating, fatigue, clammy, pale skin, and sometimes headache, nausea and vomiting, muscle cramps and fainting.
• Help the victim move to a cool, shaded area and lie down.
• Loosen or remove his or her clothing.
• Place cool, wet clothes on the forehead and wrists.
• If the victim has fainted and doesn't respond promptly, hold aromatic spirits of ammonia under his or her nose.

- If the victim is conscious, give him or her juice, soda or a flavored beverage like Gatorade.
- Make sure the victim continues to rest until fully recovered. Iced coffee or a sweet drink at this point should help hasten recovery.
- If the measures listed above don't work or if symptoms last longer than one hour, seek medical help.

HEATSTROKE
(SUNSTROKE)

This is a very serious, potentially life-threatening condition. It occurs when body temperature rises dangerously high as a result of heat exposure. Symptoms include high body temperature (above 106°F), red, hot, dry skin (no sweating), a rapid, strong pulse and, sometimes, confusion or unconsciousness.
- Move the victim into the shade.
- Using cool cloths, bathe the victim's body.
- If a fan is available, use it to blow air across the victim's body.
- If ice is available, place ice packs or ice wrapped in a cloth on the back of the victim's neck, armpits and groin area.
- If the victim is conscious, give him or her cool liquids to drink.
- If a thermometer is available, monitor the victim's body temperature and continue treatment until temperature drops below 102°F.
- Once temperature has dropped, keep the victim's body cool with wet cloths.

• Get medical help or take the victim to the nearest hospital emergency room immediately.

INSECT STINGS

Insect stings are most threatening to people who are allergic to the venom of bees, wasps and other stinging insects. However, stings can be painful to anyone and can occur when bees or other insects get trapped in automobiles. If you are allergic to insect stings, see page 31 in the section on Special Needs.

Typical symptoms of insect stings are pain, swelling, redness, itching and/or burning. If the insect was a bee, a tiny black stinger may protrude from the skin at the site of the sting. Flick or scrape it off quickly—squeezing and lifting it out will inject more venom under the skin.

After the stinger is removed, and for all other insect stings:
• Wash the affected area with soap and water.
• Cold compresses or ice will reduce discomfort and stop the venom from spreading.
• An antihistamine, calamine lotion or a paste made of baking soda and water can be soothing.
• Multiple stings can cause a more serious, toxic reaction. Symptoms include swelling, headache, muscle cramps, fever, drowsiness, unconsciousness.

• Remove the stingers as described above if the victim was stung by bees.

- Follow the other steps listed above for uncompli-
cated insect stings.
- Get medical help.
- Anyone who develops hives, breathing problems or
tightness in the throat as a result of an insect sting
needs *immediate* medical attention.

JELLYFISH STINGS
(PORTUGUESE MAN-OF-WAR)

Stings from these sea creatures can cause burning and
reddening of the skin, a rash, and, with severe reactions, muscle cramps, nausea and vomiting as well as
breathing difficulties. Victims allergic to the sting may
go into shock.
- Flush the skin with seawater.
- If a leg was stung (legs are usually the target), elevate it slightly.
- Get immediate medical attention for victims who
have severe reactions.

LIGHTNING STRIKE

Potential injuries include disorientation, dizziness,
burns, bleeding, inability to speak, shock, broken
bones. Victims may stop breathing and die.
    There is no danger in touching someone who has
been struck by lightning.
- If the victim is not breathing, maintain an open airway and restore breathing with mouth-to-mouth resuscitation (page xxxvi).

- If there is no pulse or heartbeat, perform CPR (page xxxvi).
- Administer first aid for other symptoms (bleeding, shock, broken bones, burns, etc.).
- Get medical help as quickly as possible.

SHALLOW-WATER BLACKOUT

Children are most likely to experience this problem if they hyperventilate in order to stay underwater. Under these circumstances, the victim can become unconscious due to lack of oxygen and, if not removed from the water promptly, can drown.

- Pull the victim out of the water.
- Maintain an open airway; restore breathing with mouth-to-mouth resuscitation (page xxxvi).
- Get medical help as there may be a delayed reaction that will require further treatment. (Also see Drowning, page 64.)

STINGRAYS
(WHIP RAYS)

Stingrays are fish with long, whiplike tails. They live in shallow salt water. While they are unlikely to attack, they may lash out with their tails if stepped on. The tail contains a toxin-releasing barb that can lacerate and penetrate the skin. Symptoms include a cut that is often deep and ragged, painful swelling and, occasionally, blood poisoning. Severe stings can lead to shock. Similar injuries can be inflicted by saltwater catfish, scorpion fish, toadfish and stargazers. First aid is the same.

- Wash the wound immediately with saltwater.
- Remove any part of the stinger that remains in the wound.
- Immerse the affected site in hot water for a half hour to ninety minutes; the water should be as hot as the victim can tolerate without discomfort or burning.
- Get medical attention; the victim may need a tetanus shot or an antibiotic to prevent infection.

SUNBURN

Symptoms of sunburn include skin redness and pain, although more severe burns may cause blistering and some swelling.

- Bathe the burned area with cold water.
- Mild burns may then be treated with anesthetic ointments.
- Do *not* break any blisters that develop with more severe burns. Instead, cover with a clean cloth or sterile bandage and seek medical attention.
- Use aspirin or Ibupropen to relieve pain.

SWIMMER'S ITCH

This condition is characterized by intense itching and reddened and dimpled skin. It is caused by penetration of the skin by a wormlike species known as cercariae.

- Apply cortisone lotions or ointments to relieve the itch.
- See a doctor for treatment of severe reactions; an oral antihistamine or oral cortisone drugs may be prescribed.

IN THE
WILDERNESS

▼

INDEX

FIRST-AID KIT

Flashlight
Bandages, assorted sizes
Roll sterile gauze bandage
Dozen gauze pads (4" x 4")
Waterproof adhesive tape (one roll)
Butterfly bandages
Elastic bandage (3" wide)
Absorbent cotton
Triangular bandage (for use as a sling, a large scarf can
    substitute)
Aspirin
Acetominophen (if there are children in the party)
Ipecac (one bottle, to induce vomiting)
Snakebite kit
Insect repellent
Insect spray
Hydrogen peroxide
Antihistamine
Calamine lotion
Nasal-decongestant spray or drops, one bottle

Ice pack
Hot-water bottle
Rubbing alcohol
Plain or antiseptic soap (one bar)
Thermometers (oral and rectal)
Scissors
Tweezers
Sewing needle (to remove splinters)
Safety pins (large)
Ice pack

SAFETY PRECAUTIONS

The following items should be packed with hiking and camping gear:
- Map of area
- Compass
- Flashlight plus extra batteries
- Extra clothing plus rain gear
- Sunglasses
- Sunscreen
- Pocketknife
- Matches in waterproof container
- Candle
- Water (in canteen)
- Paper and pencil (to note details of injury or symptoms of illness)
- Coins for use in pay telephones

Take the following precautions before every excursion of more than a few hours in unfamiliar territory:

- Tell someone responsible where you are going and when you expect to return.
- If you have an itinerary for a camping or hiking trip of more than a day's duration, leave the information with a responsible friend, family member, park ranger or local police.
- Make a note of the location of the nearest telephone before entering a wilderness area.
- Discuss response to emergency with others in the party; like the Boy Scouts, be prepared.

ALTITUDE SICKNESS
(MOUNTAIN SICKNESS)

Climbing to high altitudes, particularly if you ascend quickly, can lead to a number of symptoms, some quite serious. Altitude sickness is believed to stem from changes in air pressure and oxygen availability at heights of eight thousand feet or more, although symptoms can occur at five thousand feet. Many symptoms will pass once the victim becomes accustomed to the altitude, but any that are severe or persistent demand that the victim be moved to a lower altitude as quickly as possible. Symptoms include headache, weakness, fatigue, dizziness, muscle pain, shortness of breath, disturbed sleep with difficulty breathing, nausea, vomiting, fainting, disorientation, confusion, hallucinations, unconsciousness. Symptoms may take a few days to develop.

- Encourage the victim to rest and to breathe deeply and regularly.

- Give him or her something to drink. Dehydration may be a factor.
- If the victim faints or is unconscious, maintain an open airway and, if necessary, restore breathing with mouth-to-mouth resuscitation (page xxxvi).
- *Never* send anyone off alone with these or other physical symptoms. As soon as a victim with severe symptoms can be moved, return with him or her to a lower altitude.
- Seek medical treatment for victims with severe symptoms.

ANIMAL BITES

Animal bites typically result in puncture wounds. Except in unusual cases of a severe attack, the danger is not the injury itself but the possibility that the animal may be infected by rabies. In addition to dogs, wild animals including raccoons, foxes, coyotes, ground hogs, skunks and bats can carry and transmit the disease. If not detected before the onset of symptoms (typically about fifty-five days following infection), rabies is inevitably fatal. For this reason, always make every effort to capture an animal that has bitten a human. If the animal is killed, its body should be sent to health authorities for examination to determine whether or not it is infected. (Avoid injuring the animal's head; its brain must be examined for a rabies diagnosis.) Domestic live animals are watched to see if they develop symptoms. A wild animal that bites a human without provocation is presumed to be infected, and the victim will need anti-rabies vaccine. If animals are infected, any human bitten must be treated with anti-rabies serum to prevent development of the disease.

The other danger is from infection, particularly if the bite results in a deep puncture wound. The victim will need medical attention and, probably, a tetanus shot or booster.

- Clean the bite thoroughly with antiseptic soap or detergent and rinse well with water that is as hot as the victim can tolerate comfortably.
- Cover the bite with a clean cloth or sterile dressing and immobilize the area that has been injured.
- If you have been bitten by a domestic animal, get from the owner the certificate of the latest rabies shot or booster and take it with you to the doctor.
- Take the victim to the nearest hospital or doctor as quickly as possible.
- Report the bite to local health authorities, and if you have captured or killed the animal, turn it or its body over to authorities.

THE BENDS AND BAROTRAUMA
(DECOMPRESSION SICKNESS; CAISSON DISEASE)

This condition affects divers who surface too quickly from very deep water. It is caused by air bubbles of nitrogen forming in the blood and can be fatal if one of these bubbles travels to the brain. Symptoms include pain (the victim may double over), breathing difficulties, paralysis, joint pain. Bleeding from the nose and ears is related to barotrauma, a rapid expansion of compressed air upon rising from depth.

- Maintain an open airway and, if necessary, perform mouth-to-mouth resuscitation (page xxxvi) to restore breathing; if the victim's heart isn't beating or you can't find a pulse, perform CPR (page xxxv).
- Get medical help immediately.

BLISTERS

Blisters are caused by friction against the skin from shoes or clothing. They usually occur on the heel but can develop on the toes as a result of a foot sliding forward in a shoe or boot when walking downhill.

- Cover small, unopened blisters with a bandage or gauze pad.
- If a blister breaks, wash with soap and water and bandage.
- To open a large blister likely to break in the course of normal activity, wash the area with soap and water and insert a flame-sterilized needle at the lower edge. Press out the fluid gently and bandage.
- Seek medical treatment for any signs of infection: redness, pus or red streaks leading from the blister.

To prevent blisters, wear comfortable, well-fitting shoes (or boots) with stockings or socks. If you expect to hike or will be doing a lot of walking, cover areas likely to blister with moleskin or adhesive tape.

CHILLS

Chills can be a response to cold temperatures or cold water or may signify some type of infection or illness.

- Keep victims comfortable and warm. Use several blankets if possible.
- If the victim is not nauseated or vomiting, hot liquids including tea, coffee, hot chocolate or soup can be warming.
- Seek medical help if chills are followed by fever or other symptoms indicating that illness, not cold temperatures, is responsible.

DEHYDRATION

Lack of water due to excessive sweating in hot weather or loss of body fluids because of diarrhea or vomiting can lead to extreme thirst, fatigue, dizziness and abdominal or muscle cramps. Dehydration can be life-threatening, particularly among infants and the elderly.

- Move the victim into a cool, shady area.
- Give fluids to drink: water, clear broth, juice, a soft drink or flavored beverage like Gatorade. If only carbonated beverages are available, shake them to eliminate the fizz.
- Seek medical treatment for persistent symptoms or if the victim experiences nausea, diarrhea or convulsions.

DROWNING

To rescue a drowning person within reach of the shore, a pier or boat, extend a pole, an oar, rope, or other object that he or she can grasp and hold while being pulled to safety. If available, a life preserver or flotation cushion can support the victim until you are able to get close enough for rescue. Do not try to rescue someone by extending your arm or leg. You may be pulled into the water yourself.

- If the victim is not breathing, start mouth-to-mouth resuscitation (page xxxvi) at once, as soon as his or her head is out of the water; you will have to administer CPR (page xxxv) if you can't detect a pulse or heartbeat.
- Once the victim is breathing normally, watch him or her carefully for signs of shock (page 26).
- Keep the victim comfortably warm but do not give food or water.
- Seek medical attention immediately since there may be a delayed reaction that requires emergency measures. This applies to people who were breathing normally when rescued as well as to those who had to be resuscitated.
- If you suspect a back or neck injury due to a diving or surfboard accident, slide the victim out of the water onto a surfboard or other wide board that can fully support the body from head to buttocks. If no board is available, pull the victim out of the water by the armpits or legs in the direction of the length of the body. Avoid twisting the body or moving the

head in any direction although, if the victim is rescued facedown, you will have to turn him or her over carefully to perform mouth-to-mouth resuscitation or CPR (see pages xxxv–xxxvi). (Also see Shallow-Water Blackout, page 95.)

FISHHOOK INJURY

A common injury among fishermen, this occurs when a hook gets caught in the body.
- If the point of the hook has pierced the skin, slide it out in the direction of entry.
- If the hook is embedded, push it through the skin until the barb emerges.
- Clip off the end with the barb (use pliers or clippers) and back the other end out in the direction it entered the skin.
- Clean the wound with soap and water and see a doctor; the victim may need a tetanus shot.

FROSTBITE

Exposure to cold temperatures can lead to frostbite, freezing of body parts, most commonly the fingers, toes, nose and ears. Symptoms include a tingling sensation, numbness, reddened skin that later turns white.
- Remove any clothing, gloves and/or shoes that cover the frozen area.
- Warm the frozen part rapidly by immersing it, if possible, in warm (not hot) water or wrapping it in

blankets or several layers of dry clothing or towels. Never rewarm a frostbitten part in the field if there is a chance that refreezing may occur before reaching a doctor or hospital.

- Do *not* expose it to high temperatures (a fire, stove or other heating apparatus).
- Do *not* rub the frozen part with snow or anything else.
- Once skin color returns to normal and the victim feels comfortable, the frozen area should be exercised (flexing fingers or toes), but don't allow the victim to walk.
- Give the victim a warm drink.
- Separate frostbitten fingers or toes and wrap with a clean cloth or sterile gauze.
- Keep the victim warm and seek medical help for all but the most minor and transient episodes of frostbite.

HEAT CRAMPS

Heavy sweating as a result of strenuous activity can lead to heat cramps. Symptoms are muscle pain particularly in the calves or abdomen.

- Help the victim to a cool, shaded spot.
- Massage the cramped muscle.
- As long as the victim is not vomiting, give him or her fluids such as juice, soft drinks or a flavored beverage like Gatorade.

HEAT EXHAUSTION

Heat exhaustion typically occurs among people who are not used to hot weather. It affects women more often than men and is more common among those of both sexes who tend to perspire a lot.

Symptoms include heavy sweating, fatigue, clammy, pale skin, and, sometimes, headache, nausea and vomiting, muscle cramps and fainting.

- Help the victim move to a cool, shaded area and lie down.
- Loosen or remove his or her clothing.
- Place cool, wet cloths on the forehead and wrists.
- If the victim has fainted and doesn't respond promptly, hold aromatic spirits of ammonia under his or her nose.
- If the victim is conscious, give him or her fluids such as juice, soft drinks or a flavored beverage like Gatorade.
- Make sure the victim continues to rest until fully recovered. Iced coffee or a sweet drink at this point should hasten recovery.
- If the measures listed above don't work or if symptoms last longer than one hour, seek medical help.

HEATSTROKE
(SUNSTROKE)

This is a very serious, potentially life-threatening condition. It occurs when body temperature rises dangerously high as a result of heat exposure. Symptoms include high body temperature (above 106°F), red, hot, dry skin (no sweating), a rapid, strong pulse, and sometimes confusion or unconsciousness.

- Move the victim into the shade.
- Using cool cloths, bathe the victim's body.
- If a fan is available, use it to blow air across the victim's body.
- If ice is available, place ice packs or ice wrapped in a cloth on the back of the victim's neck, armpits and groin area.
- If the victim is conscious, give him or her cool liquids to drink.
- If a thermometer is available, monitor the victim's body temperature and continue treatment until temperature drops below 102°F.
- Once temperature has dropped, keep the victim's body cool with wet cloths.
- Get medical help or take the victim to the nearest hospital emergency room.

HYPOTHERMIA

Exposure to cold temperatures or wet, windy weather can cause hypothermia, chilling of the body that results in a lowering of core temperature. Symptoms include shivering, numbness and coordination problems (the victim may not be able to use his or her hands easily; striking matches or tying knots becomes difficult or awkward). Victims may be unaware of and deny a developing problem. To be safe, treat all symptoms whether or not the person perceives a problem. More severe cases of hypothermia are characterized by uncontrollable shivering, confusion, slurred speech and lethargy and, eventually, unconsciousness.

- As soon as you see signs of hypothermia developing, get the victim out of the cold and, if wet, into dry clothing.
- As long as the victim is fully conscious, offer warm liquids or food.
- If the victim has lost consciousness, maintain an open airway, and, if necessary restore breathing with mouth-to-mouth resuscitation (see page xxxvi). Then move the victim into a warm, dry area and keep warm and dry.
- Get medical help as soon as possible.
- If you are in a remote area and cannot obtain prompt medical attention, keep the victim warm with blankets, and give food and drink only if the victim is fully conscious and capable of swallowing easily.

INSECT BITES

Ticks

Two types of tick bites require medical attention. One, from the deer tick (*Ixodes dammini*), can lead to Lyme disease, a debilitating condition characterized by muscle aches and fatigue. The other, from a tick called *Dermacentor andersoni,* causes Rocky Mountain spotted fever, a potentially life-threatening disease.

Deer Ticks

Deer ticks are found in the summer in heavily wooded and grassy areas. If you know or suspect you have been bitten, see a doctor as soon as possible. You will need antibiotic treatment if you are infected.

A round, red "bull's-eye" rash usually develops at the site of the deer-tick bite.

Rocky Mountain Spotted Fever

This disease occurs throughout the United States and Canada. Symptoms include headache, fever, loss of appetite, a pink or red rash on the wrists and ankles that spreads to the arms, legs and the rest of the body; swelling around the eyes, hands and feet.

Rocky Mountain spotted fever can be treated with antibiotics if caught early. Consult your doctor for a blood test if you know or suspect you have been bitten by a tick.

To Remove a Tick

- With tweezers grasp the tick at its head and pull it off slowly. Do *not* use your fingers, a match or lighted cigarette, all of which can cause the tick or its head to become more deeply embedded.
- Clean the wound with rubbing alcohol or an antiseptic.
- If the tick's head becomes embedded in the skin, use a razor blade sterilized in flame or scrape off the skin containing the head and mouth; alterna-

tively, a sterilized needle can be used to break the
skin and remove the head or mouth.
- Clean the wound as directed above.

Preventing Tick Bites

Cover as much of your body as possible when hiking in
wooded areas. Wear shoes, socks, long trousers, long-
sleeved shirts and light-colored clothing so ticks can be
seen. Check yourself, pets, towels and clothing for ticks
after walking in wooded areas.

Spiders

Black widows are distinguished by a red hourglass-
shaped spot on their abdomens. Using an insect repellent containing DEET (N.N. diethylmetatolumide) can
reduce your risk. These spiders are found in many areas
of the United States. Their bites are serious but not
necessarily fatal. Symptoms include redness, swelling
and pain around the bite, abdominal pain, muscle
cramps, tightness in the chest.
- If necessary, maintain an open airway and restore
  breathing with mouth-to-mouth resuscitation (page
  xxxvi).
- Place an ice pack or cold compresses on the bite.
- Make sure the victim keeps the bitten area below
  his or her heart.
- Take the victim to the nearest hospital emergency
  room.

Brown recluse (fiddleback) spiders have very long
legs and violin-shaped markings on their trunks. They

are most prevalent in the South but may be found as far north as Indiana, Illinois, Missouri and Kansas. Their bites cause severe, irreversible tissue damage around the bite area. It is *vital* to get a bite victim to the nearest hospital as quickly as possible.

Symptoms include a stinging sensation, redness that turns into a blister, increasing pain, chills, fever, nausea, vomiting, rash.

- Maintain an open airway and restore breathing with mouth-to-mouth resuscitation (page xxxvi) if necessary.
- Place an ice pack or cold compresses on the bite.
- Make sure the victim keeps the bitten area below his or her heart.
- Take the victim to the nearest hospital emergency room.

Tarantula bites are less serious than those of black widow or brown recluse spiders and may not require medical treatment. The only symptom is pain, although a wound may later develop at the site of the bite.

- Wash the bitten area with soap and water and cover with an ice pack.
- Apply calamine lotion or other soothing medication.
- If a severe reaction develops, maintain an open airway and, if necessary, restore breathing with mouth-to-mouth resuscitation (page xxxvi).
- Get prompt medical attention should a severe reaction occur.

Scorpions

Although the sting of some scorpions can be deadly, most species found in the United States are not particularly threatening. The most dangerous reactions usually develop among children.

Symptoms of a scorpion bite include burning at the site of the sting, pain that extends from the sting throughout the adjacent area, headache, nausea and vomiting, muscle spasms and twitching, shock, convulsions and, possibly, coma.

- Maintain an open airway and, if necessary, restore breathing with mouth-to-mouth resuscitation (page xxxvi).
- Cover the bitten area with an ice pack or cold compresses.
- Watch for and treat any signs of shock (page 26) that develop.
- Take the victim to the nearest hospital emergency room.
- Make sure that the victim keeps the bitten area lower than his or her heart during the trip to the hospital.

LIGHTNING STRIKE

Potential injuries include disorientation, dizziness, burns, bleeding, inability to speak, shock, broken bones. Victims may stop breathing and die.

There is no danger in touching someone who has been struck by lightning.

- If the victim is not breathing, maintain an open airway and restore breathing with mouth-to-mouth resuscitation (page xxxvi).
- If you can't feel a pulse or heartbeat, perform CPR (page xxxv).
- Administer first aid for other symptoms (bleeding, shock, broken bones, burns, etc.)
- Get medical help as quickly as possible.

MUSHROOM POISONING

It is very hard to distinguish edible from poisonous mushrooms. Since several varieties can cause life-threatening illnesses, extreme caution should be exercised before picking and eating them. Initial symptoms usually occur within several hours after eating and include abdominal pain, diarrhea, vomiting. In time, a number of other more alarming symptoms may develop: breathing difficulties, sweating, excess salivation, tears, dizziness, shock, convulsions and coma.

- Induce vomiting with ipecac if available (two tablespoons for adults and children over twelve; one tablespoon for children between one and eleven years of age; two teaspoons for infants). Repeat the dose once if vomiting doesn't occur within fifteen minutes.
- If ipecac isn't available, induce vomiting by tickling the back of the throat with a finger or spoon.
- Get medical help immediately.

POISON IVY, POISON OAK, AND POISON SUMAC

Most people who come into contact with these poisonous plants develop an allergic reaction to an oily substance called urushiol they all contain. Symptoms include itching and a rash that may blister. Severe reactions may cause headache and fever.

- Remove clothing and set aside for laundering. Make sure that the garments do not come into contact with clean clothes or towels since the oil can rub off.
- Wash the skin thoroughly with soap and water as soon as possible after contact with the plant.
- Antihistamine or cortisone ointments can relieve the itching.
- Get medical help for anyone who suffers a severe reaction.

SHALLOW-WATER BLACKOUT

Children are most likely to experience this problem if they hyperventilate in order to stay underwater for longer than they could otherwise. Under these circumstances, the victim can pass out due to lack of oxygen and, if not removed from the water promptly, can drown.

- Pull the victim out of the water.
- Maintain an open airway; restore breathing with mouth-to-mouth resuscitation (page xxxvi).
- Get medical help, as there may be a delayed reac-

tion that will require further treatment. (Also see Drowning, page 84.)

SNAKEBITES

Both poisonous and nonpoisonous snakes can bite humans. Since bites from poisonous snakes can be fatal, they require prompt first aid and immediate medical attention. There are four types of poisonous snakes in the United States: rattlesnakes found throughout the country; water moccasins (cottonmouths) and copperheads found in Southeast and South Central states; and coral snakes found in the Southeast and Southwest.

After any snakebite, it is essential to determine which kind of snake was responsible since the victim may need an anti-venom shot. If possible, kill or capture the snake. If not, try to remember what it looked like. Rattlesnakes, water moccasins and copperheads have slitlike eyes, deep pits between their nostrils and eyes, and triangular-shaped heads. They leave distinctive bite marks: two puncture wounds where the fangs enter the skin and two sets of teeth marks extending backward from the puncture wound.

Rattlesnake, Water Moccasin and Copperhead Bites

Symptoms include pain, discoloration of the skin and swelling at the site of the bite; weakness, nausea and vomiting, blurred vision, breathing difficulties, convulsions and shock.

- As soon as someone is bitten, summon medical help. If you are in a remote area, you *must* take the victim to the nearest hospital emergency room as soon as possible after administering first aid.
- Maintain an open airway and restore breathing and circulation via mouth-to-mouth resuscitation and CPR (pages xxxv–xxxvi) if necessary.
- Keep the victim still and quiet.
- If the bite is on an arm or leg, place a broad, constricting band (a wide belt or strip of cloth) above the bite. It should not be so tight that you can't force your finger underneath. If the area around the band swells, move it a few inches farther up the arm or leg toward the body. Otherwise, do not move it until you get the victim to a hospital or doctor.
- Immobilize the bitten arm or leg with a splint and keep it at heart level in a natural position.
- If necessary, treat the victim for shock (page 26).
- Keep the victim still; do not let him or her move or walk (unless unavoidable to get out of danger or en route to transportation to the hospital).
- If the victim is conscious, can swallow easily and wants a drink, give him or her sips of water; do *not* give water or anything else to someone who is nauseated, vomiting or unconscious. Do *not* give alcoholic beverages.
- Do *not* attempt to suck the venom from the snakebite.
- As soon as possible after administering first aid, take the victim to the nearest hospital emergency room.

Coral Snakes

Symptoms include pain and swelling at the site of the bite, blurred vision, drooping eyelids, drooling, overwhelming drowsiness, heavy sweating, nausea and vomiting, breathing difficulties, unconsciousness.

It is *essential* to get the victim to a hospital as quickly as possible.

- Wash and immobilize the affected area.
- Keep the victim as still and quiet as possible.

(None of the other measures described above for treatment of rattlesnake, water-moccasin or copperhead bites are appropriate for coral-snake bites.)

Nonpoisonous Snakes

Clean and bandage the bite and get medical attention. The victim may need a tetanus shot.

SNOW BLINDNESS

The reflection of the sun's ultraviolet rays from snow can cause sunburn of the eye's surface. Symptoms include bloodshot, tearing, irritated or dry eyes; the sensation that there is something in the eye or that eyes feel gritty or sandy; sometimes there is pain when the eyes are moved or blinked. Symptoms usually develop after several hours of unprotected exposure. Anyone planning to travel on snow should wear sunglasses that screen out 90 percent of ultraviolet light and have side shields.

- Protect the eyes from further sun exposure.
- Cover the eyes with dark glasses or goggles that have side shields; to improvise, place adhesive tape over ordinary glasses or sunglasses leaving only a slit to allow the victim to see and bend cardboard or other similar material to form side shields if goggles are unavailable.
- Eye patches will help relieve pain, but then the victim will have to be led; this may be the only alternative in severe cases when pain is intense.
- Give the victim aspirin for pain relief and cover his or her eyes with cold, wet compresses.

SPLINTERS

The same technique is used for removing splinters of wood, slivers of glass or small bits of wire or metal.

- Sterilize tweezers or a sewing needle by holding the end over an open flame for a few moments.
- If the splinter is sticking out of the skin, grasp the protruding end with the tweezers and pull it out at the same angle that it entered.
- If the splinter is embedded in the skin but visible, use the needle to push the skin aside so you can reach the end of the splinter with the tweezers. Grasp and pull out at the angle by which it entered.
- Once the splinter is out, squeeze the spot where it punctured the skin so it will bleed slightly to wash out germs; then wash the injured area with soap and water and, if necessary, apply a bandage.
- If you can't reach a deeply embedded splinter with

the methods described above, get medical help to remove it. The victim may need a tetanus shot.
- Seek medical attention for signs of infection: redness, pus or red streaks in the skin around the wound.

SUNBURN

Symptoms of sunburn include skin redness and pain, although more severe burns may cause blistering and some swelling.
- Bathe the burned area with cold water.
- Mild burns may then be treated with anesthetic ointments.
- Do *not* break any blisters that develop with more severe burns. Instead, cover with a clean cloth or sterile bandage and seek medical attention.

SPORTS

▼

INDEX

Muscle Cramps
Plantar Fasciitis (see Heel Spur)
Runner's Knee
Shallow-Water Blackout
Shin Splints
Shoulder Separation
Skier's Thumb
Snow Blindness
Sprains
Stress Fractures
Sunburn
Sunstroke (see Heatstroke)
Swimmer's Ear (see Ear Injuries)
Swimmer's Itch
Swimmer's Shoulder
Tennis Elbow
Torn Knee Cartilage
Torn Knee Ligament

FIRST-AID KIT

Flashlight
Bandages, assorted
Roll sterile gauze bandage
Dozen gauze pads (4″ x 4″)
Butterfly bandages
Elastic bandage (3″ wide)
Adhesive tape (waterproof)
Absorbent cotton
Scissors
Tweezers
Sewing needle (for removing splinters)
Safety pins (large)
Aromatic spirits of ammonia
Aspirin
Acetominophen (if traveling with children)
Calamine lotion
Ipecac (to induce vomiting)
Antihistamine
Hydrogen peroxide
Insect repellent

Insect spray
Plain or antiseptic soap (one bar)
Rubbing alcohol

ACHILLES TENDINITIS

Injuries to the Achilles tendon that connects the calf muscles to the heel bone can stem from repetitive movement over time or from sudden stress. They can range from tiny tears that cause only mild discomfort to severe tears or even the severing of the tendon from the heel bone, which can cause intense pain. These injuries are most common among runners, people who do aerobics and those who play sports that involve running and/or sprinting. The pain occurs on the lower back of the leg.

- Stop the activity that is causing the pain.
- Apply ice to the injured area as soon as possible.
- Take aspirin or ibuprofen to reduce the pain and inflammation (providing that you do not react adversely to these drugs).
- See a doctor if the pain prevents you from walking or climbing stairs; severe injuries to the Achilles tendon may require surgical repair.
- Do not resume the exercise that led to the injury until you are pain-free; you may need physical therapy to strengthen your calf muscles and stretch the Achilles tendon.

ALTITUDE SICKNESS
(MOUNTAIN SICKNESS)

Climbing to high altitudes, particularly if you ascend quickly, can lead to a number of symptoms, some quite serious. Altitude sickness is believed to stem from changes in air pressure and oxygen availability at heights of eight thousand feet or more, although symptoms can occur at five thousand feet. Many symptoms will pass once the victim becomes accustomed to the altitude, but any that are severe or persistent demand that the victim be moved to a lower altitude as quickly as possible. Symptoms include headache, weakness, fatigue, dizziness, muscle pain, shortness of breath, disturbed sleep with difficulty breathing, nausea, vomiting, fainting, disorientation, confusion, hallucinations, unconsciousness.

- Have the victim rest and encourage him or her to breathe deeply and regularly.
- Offer something to drink, as dehydration may be a factor.
- If the victim faints or is unconscious, maintain an open airway and, if necessary, restore breathing with mouth-to-mouth resuscitation (page xxxvi).
- As soon as a victim with severe symptoms can be moved, return with him or her to a lower altitude. *Never* send someone off alone with this or other physical symptoms.
- Seek medical treatment for victims with severe symptoms.

BASEBALL FINGER

Sudden force at the end of a finger from throwing or hitting a baseball can tear a tendon. Symptoms include pain, swelling and bruising.

- Apply an ice pack to the finger as soon as possible.
- See a doctor about the need for a splint to immobilize the finger and speed healing.
- Unless you have adverse reactions to them, take aspirin or ibuprofen to relieve pain and reduce inflammation.

THE BENDS AND BAROTRAUMA
(DECOMPRESSION SICKNESS; CAISSON DISEASE)

This condition affects divers who surface too quickly from very deep water. It is caused by air bubbles of nitrogen forming in the blood and can be fatal if one of these bubbles travels to the brain. Symptoms include pain (the victim may double over), breathing difficulties, paralysis, joint pain.

Bleeding from the nose and ears usually is related to barotrauma, a rapid expansion of compressed air upon rising from depth.

- Maintain an open airway and, if necessary, perform mouth-to-mouth resuscitation (page xxxvi) to restore breathing; if the victim's heart isn't beating or you can't find a pulse, perform CPR (page xxxv).
- Get medical help immediately.

BLACK EYES

These common injuries stem from blows to the eyes with a ball or other direct physical contact. Symptoms include pain and reddened skin that later turns black and blue and eventually fades to yellow. Sometimes, a lump develops at the point of injury.

Treat first with frequent applications of cold compresses or ice. After forty-eight hours, switch to moist heat (a warm, wet washcloth or other compress).

Seek medical treatment for black eyes that are very painful, if there is severe swelling or vision problems.

- See a doctor promptly to make sure there is no bleeding in the eye or that no other complications are developing.

BLISTERS

Blisters are caused by friction against the skin from shoes or clothing. They usually occur on the heel, but can develop on the toes as a result of a foot sliding forward in a shoe or boot when walking downhill.

- Cover small, unopened blisters with a bandage or gauze pad.
- If a blister breaks, wash with soap and water and bandage.
- To open a large blister likely to break in the course of normal activity, wash the area with soap and water and insert a flame-sterilized needle at the lower edge. Press out the fluid gently and bandage.

- Seek medical treatment for any signs of infection: redness, pus or red streaks leading from the blister.

To prevent blisters, wear comfortable, well-fitting shoes (or boots) with stockings or socks. If you expect to hike or will be doing a lot of walking, cover areas likely to blister with moleskin or adhesive tape.

BRUISES

These common injuries are caused by blows. Symptoms include pain and reddened skin that later turns black and blue and eventually fades to yellow. Sometimes a lump develops at the point of injury.

Treat initially with cold compresses or ice. After forty-eight hours, switch to moist heat (a warm, wet washcloth or other compress).

Seek medical treatment for bruises that are very painful or when severe swelling develops.

BUMPS

Bumps on the head or lumps that develop elsewhere on the body due to sports-related injuries usually are not serious, but since even apparently minor head injuries can be dangerous, seek medical attention should any of the following symptoms develop after a bump on the head: bleeding from the ears, nose or mouth; unconsciousness; severe headache; vision problems, breathing difficulties; vomiting; slurred speech; confusion;

aggressive behavior or irritability; convulsions. Otherwise:
- Apply an ice pack or cold compresses to the injured area as soon as possible.

CHILLS

Chills can be a response to cold temperatures or cold water or may signify some type of infection or illness.
- Keep victims comfortable and warm. Use several blankets if possible.
- If the victim is not nauseated or vomiting, hot liquids including tea, coffee, hot chocolate or soup can be warming.
- Seek medical help if chills are followed by fever or other symptoms indicating that illness, not cold temperatures, are responsible.

DEHYDRATION

Lack of water due to excessive sweating in hot weather or loss of body fluids because of diarrhea or vomiting can lead to extreme thirst, fatigue, dizziness and abdominal or muscle cramps. Dehydration can be life-threatening, particularly among infants and the elderly.
- Move the victim into a cool, shady area.
- Give fluids to drink: water with one-half teaspoon of salt per eight ounces or clear broth. If only carbonated beverages are available, shake them to eliminate the fizz.

- Seek medical treatment for persistent symptoms or if the victim experiences nausea, diarrhea or convulsions.

DISLOCATIONS

Vigorous physical activity can cause bone dislocations in the shoulder, hip, elbow, fingers, thumb, toes and kneecap. Symptoms include swelling, tenderness, an obvious deformity in the affected joint, pain with movement, discolored skin around the site of injury.
- Help the victim into a comfortable position.
- Immobilize the injured area with a splint much as you would for a broken bone (see page 9). Don't try to put a dislocated bone back in place; you may make matters worse.
- Take the victim to the nearest hospital emergency room.

DROWNING

To rescue a drowning person within reach of the shore, a pier or boat, extend a pole, an oar, rope, or other object that he or she can grasp and hold while being pulled to safety. If available, a life preserver or flotation cushion can support the victim until you are able to get close enough for rescue. Do not try to rescue someone by extending your arm or leg. You may be pulled in yourself.
- If the victim is not breathing, start mouth-to-mouth resuscitation (page xxxvi) at once, as soon as his or

her head is out of the water; you will have to administer CPR (page xxxv) if you can't detect a pulse or heartbeat.

- Once the victim is breathing normally, watch him or her carefully for signs of shock (page 26).
- Keep the victim comfortably warm but do not give food or water.
- Seek medical attention immediately since there may be a delayed reaction that requires emergency measures. This applies to people who were breathing normally when rescued as well as those who had to be resuscitated.
- If you suspect a back or neck injury due to a diving or surfboard accident, slide the victim out of the water onto a surfboard or other wide board that can fully support the body from head to buttocks. If no board is available, pull the victim out of the water by the armpits or legs in the direction of the length of the body. Avoid twisting the body or moving the head in any direction, although, if the victim is rescued facedown, you will have to turn him or her over carefully to perform mouth-to-mouth resuscitation or CPR (pages xxxv–xxxvi). (Also see Shallow-Water Blackout, page 124).

EAR INJURIES

Diving and waterskiing accidents can lead to ear injuries, and swimming in unclean water can trigger an infection called ''swimmer's ear.''

Symptoms of ear injury include bleeding from the ear, pain and hearing loss.

- If a head injury has occurred, treat that first according to the instructions on page 21.
- Do not try to stem the flow of blood from the ear; do not insert cotton packing or anything else.
- Cover the ear with a clean cloth or bandage to prevent blood from dripping.
- Have the victim lie down so that the injured ear is toward the ground and can drain (however, do not move anyone who has suffered a serious head, neck or back injury).
- Get medical help.

Swimmer's Ear

Symptoms include pain, itching and, sometimes, a discharge from the ear.

- See a doctor promptly; the infection causing the symptoms will require treatment with an antibiotic.
- Do not insert anything in the ear.

FISHHOOK INJURY

A common injury among fishermen, this occurs when a hook gets caught in the body.

- If the point of the hook has pierced the skin, slide it out in the direction of entry.
- If the hook is embedded, push it through the skin until the barb emerges.

- Clip off the end with the barb (use pliers or clippers) and back the other end out in the direction it entered the skin.
- Clean the wound with soap and water and see a doctor; the victim may need a tetanus shot.

FOOT PAIN

Improperly fitting shoes and stress on the feet can cause a condition called Morton's neuroma, a swelling of a nerve between two bones in the forefoot. Symptoms include pain on the top of the foot, in the ball of the foot or toes. Sometimes the toes become numb. Pain can be so severe that victims can no longer participate in their sports.
- Remove shoes.
- Apply ice to the painful area.
- Elevate the foot.
- Unless you have an adverse reaction, take aspirin or ibuprofen to relieve pain and reduce inflammation.
- Get medical attention for severe pain, numb toes or pain when walking.

FROSTBITE

Exposure to cold temperatures can lead to frostbite, freezing of body parts, most commonly the fingers, toes, nose and ears. Symptoms include a tingling sensation, numbness, reddened skin that later turns white.

- Remove any clothing, gloves and/or shoes that cover the frozen area.
- Warm the frozen part rapidly by immersing it, if possible, in warm (not hot) water or wrapping it in blankets or several layers of dry clothing or towels. Never rewarm a frozen part if there is a chance of refreezing before you can get the victim to a doctor or hospital.
- Do *not* expose it to high temperatures (a fire, stove or other heating apparatus).
- Do *not* rub the frozen part with snow or anything else.
- Once skin color returns to normal and the victim feels comfortable, the frozen area should be exercised (flexing fingers or toes), but don't allow the victim to walk.
- Give the victim a warm drink.
- Separate frostbitten fingers or toes and wrap with a clean cloth or sterile gauze.
- Keep the victim warm and seek medical help for all but the most minor and transient episodes of frostbite. (Also see Hypothermia, page 120.)

GOLFER'S ELBOW

An improper downward stroke in golf or poor forehand stroke in tennis can cause inflammation or a small tear in a tendon that attaches to muscles in the inside of the forearm. Symptoms include pain on the inside of the elbow that may occur only when lifting or carrying something heavy.

- Stop any activity that causes pain.
- Apply an ice pack as soon as possible after the injury.
- See a doctor if the elbow can't be bent or straightened without pain.
- Unless you have an adverse reaction, take aspirin or ibuprofen to relieve pain and reduce inflammation.

HEAT CRAMPS

Heavy sweating as a result of strenuous activity can lead to heat cramps. Symptoms are muscle pain, particularly in the calves or abdomen.
- Help the victim to a cool, shaded spot.
- Massage the cramped muscle.
- As long as the victim is not vomiting, give him or her juice, soft drinks or a flavored beverage like Gatorade.

HEAT EXHAUSTION

Heat exhaustion typically occurs among people who are not used to hot weather. It affects women more often than men and is more common among those of both sexes who tend to perspire a lot.

Symptoms include heavy sweating, fatigue, clammy, pale skin and sometimes headache, nausea and vomiting, muscle cramps and fainting.

- Help the victim move to a cool, shaded area and lie down.
- Loosen or remove his or her clothing.
- Place cool, wet cloths on the forehead and wrists.
- If the victim has fainted and doesn't respond promptly, hold aromatic spirits of ammonia under his or her nose.
- If the victim is conscious, give him or her juice, soft drinks or a flavored beverage like Gatorade.
- Make sure the victim continues to rest until fully recovered. Iced coffee or a sweet drink at this point should help hasten recovery.
- If the measures listed above don't work or if symptoms last longer than one hour, seek medical help.

HEATSTROKE
(SUNSTROKE)

This is a very serious, potentially life-threatening condition. It occurs when body temperature rises dangerously high as a result of heat exposure. Symptoms include high body temperature (above 106°F), red, hot, dry skin (no sweating), a rapid, strong pulse and sometimes confusion or unconsciousness.

- Move the victim into the shade.
- Using cool, not ice-cold, water, bathe the victim's body.
- If available, use a fan to blow air across the victim's body.
- If ice is available, place ice packs or ice wrapped in

a cloth on the back of the victim's neck, armpits and groin area.
- If the victim is conscious, give him or her cool liquids to drink.
- If a thermometer is available, monitor the victim's body temperature and continue treatment until temperature drops below 102°F.
- Once temperature has dropped, keep the victim's body cool with wet cloths.
- Get medical help or take the victim to the nearest hospital emergency room.

HEEL SPUR
(PLANTAR FASCIITIS)

Overuse, poor arches, improper shoes or running on cement or other unyielding surfaces can give rise to heel spurs, an injury to the connective tissue on the bottom of the foot. Symptoms include pain in the heel, pain when walking (but not while running), bruising, swelling, the sensation of walking with a pebble in a shoe.
- Stop the activity that is causing pain.
- Apply an ice pack to the injured foot.
- Unless you have an adverse reaction, take aspirin or ibuprofen to relieve pain and reduce inflammation.
- Victims who can't place pressure on the affected foot while walking should get medical attention.
- Rest the foot (no running) for three to six weeks. After healing, victims may need to learn exercises to stretch the plantar fascia.

HIP POINTER

This is a bruise or tear in the muscle that attaches to the top of the ilium bone at the waist. It occurs among those who play contact sports. Symptoms are pain and, later, bruising.

- Apply an ice pack or cold compresses to the injured area as soon as possible.
- Unless you have an adverse reaction, take aspirin or ibuprofen to reduce inflammation and relieve pain.
- See a doctor if pain is so severe that walking is affected.

HYPOTHERMIA

Exposure to cold temperatures or wet, windy weather can cause hypothermia, chilling of the body that results in a lowering of core temperature. Symptoms include shivering, numbness and coordination problems (the victim may not be able to use his or her hands easily; striking matches or tying knots becomes difficult or awkward). Victims may be unaware of and deny a developing problem. To be safe, treat all symptoms whether or not the person perceives a problem. More severe cases of hypothermia are characterized by uncontrollable shivering, confusion, slurred speech and lethargy and eventually unconsciousness.

- As soon as you see signs of hypothermia develop-

ing, get the victim out of the cold and, if wet, into dry clothing.
- As long as the victim is fully conscious, offer warm liquids or food.
- If the victim has lost consciousness, maintain an open airway and if necessary, restore breathing with mouth-to-mouth resuscitation (see page xxxvi). Then, move the victim into a warm, dry area and keep warm and dry.
- Get medical help as soon as possible.
- If you are in a remote area and cannot obtain prompt medical attention, keep the victim warm with blankets and give food and drink only if the victim is fully conscious and capable of swallowing easily. (Also see Frostbite, page 115.)

KNOCKED-OUT TOOTH

- Have the victim bite down on a piece of clean, folded cloth to stop the bleeding.
- If the victim is a small child who has lost a "baby tooth," there is no need to save the tooth. If a permanent tooth is involved, find it and wrap it in a cool, wet cloth or put it in a container of whole, *not* skim, milk.
- Rush both the victim and tooth to the nearest dentist or hospital emergency room.

LIGHTNING STRIKE

Potential injuries include disorientation, dizziness, burns, bleeding, inability to speak, shock, broken bones. Victims may stop breathing and die.

There is no danger in touching someone who has been struck by lightning.

- If the victim is not breathing, maintain an open airway and restore breathing with mouth-to-mouth resuscitation (page xxxvi).
- If you can't feel a pulse or heartbeat, perform CPR (pages xxxv–xxxvi).
- Administer first aid for other symptoms (bleeding, shock, broken bones, burns, etc.).
- Get medical help as quickly as possible.

LOW-BACK PAIN

Repetitive motions or sudden force can cause muscle strains or tears or injury to a disk in the spine. Symptoms include a dull ache or sharp pain in the lower back, stiffness and general achiness.

- Get immediate medical attention for pain that is severe and radiates down the legs, for numbness or tingling in the lower back or legs and for any bowel or bladder abnormalities. These symptoms may be associated with nerve damage due to an injured vertebral disk.
- Apply ice to the back if the injury appears to be a muscle pull or tear.

- Apply heat with a heating pad, to relieve stiffness due to fatigue.
- Unless you have an adverse reaction, take aspirin or ibuprofen to relieve pain and reduce inflammation.

MUSCLE CRAMPS

Muscle cramps are a symptom of overuse—too much physical activity. They can be very painful and, initially, may worsen at rest.
- Massage the cramped muscle.
- Apply heat.
- If cramping isn't relieved by massage and heat, take the victim to a hospital emergency room.
- Unless you have an adverse reaction, take aspirin or ibuprofen to relieve pain and reduce inflammation.

RUNNER'S KNEE

An increasingly common injury, runner's knee usually stems from wear and tear on the knee, but it can develop as a result of stress such as a change in running habits, shoes, carrying weights, etc. The primary symptom is a dull ache or sharp pain around the kneecap, or pain when bending the knee to sit, squat, walk up or downstairs. There may be muscle weakness in the quadriceps (the front of the thigh) and a grinding and popping sound in the knees.

- Stop moving and rest.
- Apply ice to the injured knee.
- Unless you have an adverse reaction, take aspirin or ibuprofen to relieve pain and reduce inflammation.
- Do not resume running until completely healed; this will take from three to six weeks.

SHALLOW-WATER BLACKOUT

Children are most likely to experience this problem if they hyperventilate in order to stay underwater. Under these circumstances, the victim can become unconscious due to lack of oxygen and, if not removed from the water promptly, can drown.
- Pull the victim out of the water.
- Maintain an open airway; restore breathing with mouth-to-mouth resuscitation (page xxxvi).
- Get medical help, as there may be a delayed reaction that will require further treatment. (Also see Drowning, page 112)

SHIN SPLINTS

Shin splints are injuries to the lower front of the leg. They can be caused by a tiny tear in the muscle at a point where it attaches to the bone, a stress fracture (see page 127) or a tear or inflammation in the membrane that covers the bone surface. Sometimes, overdevelopment of muscles in the area results in restricted blood flow. Whatever the cause, the principal symptom is pain in the shin, the lower front part of the leg and, sometimes, swelling.

- Stop the activity causing the pain and do not resume until symptoms disappear.
- Apply cold compresses or an ice pack to the painful area of the leg.
- Continue using the ice pack or cold compresses at least once a day for two to four days until swelling, if any, subsides; then switch to heat (use a heating pad).
- Unless you have an adverse reaction, take aspirin or ibuprofen to reduce inflammation and relieve the pain.
- If the pain is severe enough to interfere with walking, see a doctor.

SHOULDER SEPARATION

A blow or fall can cause a tear in ligaments that hold the collarbone to the shoulder. The injury is most common in contact sports, particularly football. Symptoms include pain, difficulty moving the shoulder, swelling and bruising.

- Apply ice to the injured shoulder.
- Get prompt medical attention.

SKIER'S THUMB

This injury usually occurs when skiers fall and the ski pole forces the thumb away from the fingers, tearing or severing the ligament that attaches the thumb to the bones in the palm. Catching a ball can cause similar symptoms: pain at the base of the thumb, swelling and, later, bruising.

- Apply an ice pack to the injured thumb.
- Unless you have an adverse reaction, take aspirin or ibuprofen to relieve pain and reduce inflammation.
- See a doctor about the need for a splint to immobilize the thumb and speed healing.

SNOW BLINDNESS

The reflection of the sun's ultraviolet rays from snow can cause sunburn of the eye's surface. Symptoms include bloodshot, tearing, irritated or dry eyes; the sensation that there is something in the eye or that the eyes feel gritty or sandy; sometimes there is pain when the eyes are moved or blinked. Symptoms usually develop after several hours of unprotected exposure. Anyone planning to travel on snow should wear sunglasses that screen out 90 percent of ultraviolet light and have side shields.

- Protect the eyes from further sun exposure.
- Cover the eyes with dark glasses or goggles that have side shields; to improvise, place adhesive tape over ordinary glasses or sunglasses, leaving only a slit to allow the victim to see and bend cardboard or other similar material to form side shields if goggles are unavailable.
- Eye patches will help relieve pain, but then the vic-

tim will have to be led; this may be the only alternative in severe cases when pain is intense.
- Give the victim aspirin for pain relief and cover his or her eyes with cold, wet compresses.

SPRAINS

Any athletic activity can result in sprained ankles, an injury to one or both ligaments on the outside of the ankle. Sprains can also occur in the arms or legs. Symptoms include pain, swelling and bruising. If a leg or ankle is sprained, the victim may not be able to walk. In some cases, symptoms don't appear until hours after the injury.
- Stop and rest.
- Apply an ice pack as soon as possible.
- If a leg or ankle is injured, elevate above the level of the heart.
- If the wrist, elbow or shoulder is injured, place the affected arm in a sling.
- Get medical attention to confirm that the injury is a sprain and not a broken bone.
- Unless you have an adverse reaction, take aspirin or ibuprofen to relieve pain and reduce inflammation.

STRESS FRACTURES

Stress fractures are hairline cracks that develop in the foot or the lower leg as a result of repetitive motion, such as running or sudden stress. They are common injuries among runners, baseball, basketball and tennis players. People who walk regularly for physical exercise are also susceptible. Symptoms include pain at the point of the fracture, a burning sensation.

- Apply an ice pack to the injured area.
- Get medical attention when pain is severe or walking is affected.
- Unless you have an adverse reaction, take aspirin or ibuprofen to relieve pain and reduce inflammation.

SUNBURN

Symptoms of sunburn include skin redness and pain, although more severe burns may cause blistering and some swelling.

- Bathe the burned area with cold water.
- Mild burns may then be treated with anesthetic ointments.
- Do *not* break any blisters that develop with more severe burns. Instead, cover with a clean cloth or sterile bandage and seek medical attention.

SWIMMER'S ITCH

This condition is characterized by intense itching and reddened and dimpled skin. It is caused by penetration of the skin by a wormlike species known as cercariae.

- Apply cortisone lotions or ointments to relieve the itch.
- See a doctor for treatment of severe reactions; an oral antihistamine or oral cortisone drugs may be prescribed.

SWIMMER'S SHOULDER

The repetitive arm movements of swimming can cause strain and small tears in the muscle on top of the shoulder between the neck and the top of the arm or in other muscles supporting the shoulder. The injury also occurs among other athletes who repeat the same arm movements when playing their sport. Among them are baseball pitchers, football quarterbacks, tennis players, golfers. Symptoms include pain on top of and in front of the shoulder, pain when extending the arm forward or upward, limitation of shoulder movement.

- Apply an ice pack or cold compresses to the injured shoulder.
- Get medical attention if the arm can't be raised above the head, can't be moved at all or if there is severe pain or weakness.
- Unless you have an adverse reaction, take aspirin or ibuprofen to relieve pain and reduce inflammation.

TENNIS ELBOW

A poor backhand can cause inflammation or small tears in the tendons connecting the muscles that run along the outside of the forearm. Repetitive motions among other athletes can cause a similar injury. Those who play racquetball, paddle tennis and golf can be affected, as can bowlers, archers and skiers. Symptoms include pain on the outside of the elbow that may limit such movements as shaking hands, holding a cup, turning a knob.

- Apply an ice pack to the injured elbow.
- Unless you have an adverse reaction, take aspirin or ibuprofen to relieve pain and reduce inflammation.
- Victims who can't extend their arms forward should seek medical attention.

TORN KNEE CARTILAGE

Twisting the knee or taking a blow to the knee can result in a torn cartilage. Those who play contact sports are most susceptible, but the injury can occur among all athletes, amateur or professional. Symptoms include pain where the bones of the leg join to form the knee, swelling, a popping sound when the injury occurs and a locking or buckling of the knee.

- Rest.
- Apply an ice pack or cold compresses as soon as possible after the injury.
- Unless you have an adverse reaction, take aspirin or ibuprofen to relieve pain and reduce swelling.
- Get medical attention; severe tears may require surgical repair.

TORN KNEE LIGAMENT

An injury to one of the two ligaments that crisscross the knee can stem from a blow to the knee or from stress to the knee during strenuous athletic activity. Symptoms include pain and stiffness, neither of which may be apparent for hours after the injury. Sometimes the knee goes out of place.

- Rest.
- Apply an ice pack or cold compresses.
- Unless you have an adverse reaction, take aspirin or ibuprofen to relieve pain and reduce inflammation.
- Get medical attention; severe injuries may require surgical repair.

PART VII

TRAVELING ABROAD

▼

INDEX

FIRST-AID KIT

Assorted bandages
Dozen gauze pads (4″ x 4″)
Roll waterproof adhesive tape
Butterfly bandages
Absorbent cotton
Scissors
Tweezers
Safety pins (large)
Sewing needle (for removing splinters)
Aromatic spirits of ammonia
Acetominophen
Aspirin
Ipecac (one bottle, to induce vomiting)
Calamine lotion
Hydrogen peroxide (one small bottle)
Antihistamine
Plain or antiseptic soap (one bar)
Thermometer
Motion-sickness pills
Matches

Nasal-decongestant drops or spray
If itinerary warrants:
- Snakebite kit
- Insect repellent
- Flashlight (if you will be driving)

IMMUNIZATIONS

The only current immunization requirements are imposed by those countries where yellow fever and sometimes cholera are a threat. Smallpox vaccinations are no longer required for international travel.

The following countries require an international certificate of vaccination against yellow fever from travelers arriving directly from the United States:

Benin, Burkina Faso (formerly Upper Volta), Cameroon, Central African Republic, Congo, Côte d'Ivoire (formerly Ivory Coast), French Guiana, Gabon, Ghana, Liberia, Mali, Mauritania (only for those planning to stay more than two weeks), Niger, Rwanda, São Tomé and Príncipe (for a stay of more than two weeks), Senegal, Togo.

Yellow-fever vaccinations must be given at centers designated by each state's health department. Vaccinations against cholera can be obtained from private physicians, but the certificate of vaccination must be validated at a city, county or state health department or from physicians who possess a "uniform stamp."

No vaccinations are required to return to the United States.

Some countries require yellow-fever and/or cholera

vaccination(s) for travelers arriving from countries experiencing outbreaks of these diseases. The U.S. Centers for Disease Control publishes a biweekly summary listing of countries where these diseases are occurring. It is available by subscription to health departments, physicians, travel agencies, international airlines and other agencies dealing with international travel. Your travel agent, city, state or county health department should be able to provide current information on vaccination requirements for all countries on your itinerary. Some company health services will supply this information. If not, contact the Division of Quarantine, Centers for Disease Control, Atlanta, Georgia 30333.

HEALTH HINTS FOR TRAVELERS

- If you have any chronic health problem, wear an appropriate MedicAlert tag or bracelet; carry a wallet card containing the same information as the MedicAlert tag. (See page 30 for information on obtaining MedicAlert identification.)
- Carry an extra supply of all prescription medications you take plus a note from your physician explaining any major health problems and dosages of your medications.
- Carry an extra pair of glasses.
- Contact the American embassy or nearest consulate for referrals to local doctors who speak English.
- Check with your travel agent or local health department in advance of travel to tropical areas about the malaria risk and, if it is high, consult your doc-

tor about the advisability of taking preventive drugs.

- Be aware of the risk of contracting AIDS from blood transfusions in countries where blood is not systematically screened. You cannot take a supply of your own blood with you or have it shipped, but plasma expanders often can be substituted for blood transfusions.
- Handicapped travelers can get a free guide to services and facilities for the disabled at 472 airports worldwide. The guide, *Access Travel: A Guide to Accessibility of Terminals,* is available from the Architectural and Transportation Barriers Compliance Board, 1111 18th Street, N.W., Suite 50, Washington, D.C. 20036-3894; telephone (202) 653-7834.
- Haitian goatskin handicrafts cannot be brought into the United States because they have been found to contain spores of the bacteria that cause anthrax, an infectious disease that affects cattle and sheep and is transmissible to humans. In humans, anthrax causes flulike symptoms in its early stages. It can be treated with antibiotics but can be fatal if not carefully diagnosed and treated promptly.
- The risk of contracting sexually transmitted diseases including AIDS is high in certain areas of the world. Gonorrhea that is resistant to antibiotic treatment is prevalent in the Philippines, South Korea, Singapore, Thailand, Ghana, Kenya, Nigeria and Côte d'Ivoire, and incidence is increasing in the Caribbean and Central and South America.
- Because some countries do not limit the sale of

potentially hazardous drugs, the U.S. Public Health Service advises travelers against buying unfamiliar over-the-counter products.

ALTITUDE SICKNESS
(MOUNTAIN SICKNESS)

Climbing to high altitudes, particularly if you ascend quickly, can lead to a number of symptoms, some quite serious. Altitude sickness is believed to stem from changes in air pressure and oxygen availability at heights of eight thousand feet or more, although symptoms can occur at five thousand feet. Many symptoms will pass once the victim becomes accustomed to the atltitude, but any that are severe or persistent demand that the victim be moved to a lower altitude as quickly as possible. Symptoms include headache, weakness, fatigue, dizziness, muscle pain, shortness of breath, disturbed sleep with difficulty breathing, nausea, vomiting, fainting, disorientation, confusion, hallucinations, unconsciousness. Symptoms may take a few days to develop.

- Encourage the victim to rest and to breathe deeply and regularly.
- Give him or her something to drink. Dehydration may be a factor.
- If the victim faints or is unconscious, maintain an open airway and, if necessary, restore breathing with mouth-to-mouth resuscitation (page xxxvi).
- As soon as a victim with severe symptoms can be moved, return with him or her to a lower altitude.

Never send anyone off alone with these or other physical symptoms.
- Seek medical treatment for victims with severe symptoms.

ANIMAL BITES

Animal bites typically result in puncture wounds. Except in unusual cases of a severe attack, the danger is not the injury itself but the possibility that the animal may be infected by rabies. In addition to dogs, wild animals including raccoons, foxes, coyotes, groundhogs, skunks and bats may be infected and can transmit the disease. If not detected before the onset of symptoms (typically about fifty-five days following infection), rabies is inevitably fatal. For this reason, always make every effort to capture an animal that has bitten a human. If the animal is killed, its body should be sent to health authorities for examination to determine whether or not it is infected. Avoid injuring the animal's head; its brain is needed for rabies diagnosis. Domestic animals are watched to see if they develop symptoms. Any wild animal that bites a human without provocation is presumed to be infected and the victim will need anti-rabies vaccine. If animals are infected, any human bitten must be treated with anti-rabies serum to prevent development of the disease.

There is also a danger of infection, particularly if the bite results in a deep puncture wound. The victim may need a tetanus shot or booster.

- Clean the bite thoroughly with antiseptic soap or detergent, and rinse well with water that is as hot as the victim can tolerate comfortably.
- Cover the bite with a clean cloth or sterile dressing and immobilize the area that has been injured.
- Take the victim to the nearest hospital or doctor as quickly as possible.
- If you have been bitten by a domestic animal and can locate and communicate with the owner, determine whether the animal has had a rabies shot and, if so, whether documentation is available. If it is, take it with you to the doctor.
- Report the bite to the local health authorities and, if you have captured or killed the animal, turn it or its body over to authorities for testing.

BLISTERS

Blisters are caused by friction against the skin from shoes or clothing. They usually occur on the heel, but can develop on the toes as a result of a foot sliding forward in a shoe or boot when walking downhill.

- Cover small, unopened blisters with a bandage or gauze pad.
- If a blister breaks, wash with soap and water and bandage.
- To open a large blister likely to break in the course of normal activity, wash the area with soap and water and insert a flame-sterilized needle at the lower edge. Press out the fluid gently and bandage.

- Seek medical treatment for any signs of infection: redness, pus or red streaks leading away from the blister.

To prevent blisters, wear comfortable, well-fitting shoes (or boots) with stockings or socks. If you expect to hike or will be doing a lot of walking, cover areas likely to blister with moleskin or adhesive tape.

DIARRHEA

Between 20 and 50 percent of all persons who travel abroad experience some degree of traveler's diarrhea caused by eating contaminated food or drinking contaminated water. The problem is more common among visitors to the developing countries of Latin America, Africa, the Middle East and Asia, but can occur anywhere sanitation is poor. Symptoms include frequent loose stools sometimes accompanied by abdominal cramps, nausea, bloating, fever and vomiting. Diarrhea usually begins abruptly during travel or soon after return home. Most cases clear up on their own after three to four days, but some can continue for a week or more.

To prevent traveler's diarrhea, *avoid* raw meat and seafood, uncooked vegetables, salads and fruits, tap water, ice and unpasteurized dairy products. It is usually *safe* to drink beer, wine, coffee, tea and other beverages made with boiled water. Carbonated beverages are usually safe, but in some countries they are bottled under unsanitary conditions. You are least likely to encounter contaminated food or water when eating in private homes or restaurants. You are less safe with food or drink purchased from street peddlers.

Treatment:

- Drink plenty of liquids. (Since dairy products can aggravate diarrhea, they should be avoided.)
- Pepto-Bismol or the drugs Lomotil or Imodium often can provide relief. Lomotil requires a prescription. Imodium is available over the counter or by prescription.
- Certain types of traveler's diarrhea can be treated with antibiotics.
- Get medical attention when diarrhea persists for more than a week or if there is blood in the stool.
- Infants and children are more likely than adults to become dehydrated as a result of diarrhea. They should not be given solid food. Offer juice, weak tea, clear soup or carbonated beverages that have been shaken to eliminate the fizz.
- Get medical attention for any infant or child who has frequent and persistent diarrhea (more than three loose, watery stools within four to six hours). Fever, a dry mouth, vomiting, drowsiness, less frequent urination or blood in the stool also require medical attention.

HEAT CRAMPS

Heavy sweating as a result of strenuous activity can lead to heat cramps. Symptoms are muscle pain, particularly in the calves or abdomen.

- Help the victim to a cool, shaded spot.
- Massage the cramped muscle.
- As long as the victim is not vomiting, give him or her saltwater to drink (one-half teaspoon of salt per eight ounces of water) or salt tablets, if available.

HEAT EXHAUSTION

Heat exhaustion typically occurs among people who are not used to hot weather. It affects women more often than men and is more common among those of both sexes who tend to perspire a lot.

Symptoms include heavy sweating, fatigue, clammy, pale skin and sometimes headache, nausea and vomiting, muscle cramps and fainting.

- Help the victim move to a cool, shaded area and lie down.
- Loosen or remove his or her clothing.
- Place cool, wet cloths on the forehead and wrists.
- If the victim has fainted and doesn't respond promptly, hold aromatic spirits of ammonia under his or her nose.
- If the victim is conscious, give him or her juice, a soft drink or flavored beverage.
- Make sure the victim continues to rest until fully recovered. Iced coffee or a sweet drink at this point should help hasten recovery.
- If the measures listed above don't work or if symptoms last longer than one hour, seek medical help.

HEATSTROKE
(SUNSTROKE)

This is a very serious, potentially life-threatening condition. It occurs when body temperature rises dangerously high as a result of heat exposure. Symptoms include high body temperature (above 106°F), red, hot, dry skin (no sweating), a rapid, strong pulse and sometimes confusion or unconsciousness.

- Try to lower body temperature by immersing the victim in cool water or bathing with cool cloths.
- If available, use a fan to blow air across the victim's body.
- Monitor body temperature with a thermometer and continue treatment until temperature drops below 102°F.
- Once temperature has dropped, keep the victim's body cool with wet cloths.
- Get medical help or take the victim to the nearest hospital emergency room.

INSECT STINGS
(MOSQUITO BITES)

Travelers to mosquito-infested areas should take the following precautions:

- Remain in well-screened areas during the hours when mosquitos feed.
- Use mosquito nets for sleeping.
- Wear clothes that cover most of the body.

- Spray exposed skin with an insect repellent containing Deet (N.N. diethylmetatoluamide).
- Spray living and sleeping quarters with flying-insect spray containing pyrethrum.

The following diseases are transmitted by mosquitoes:

Dengue Fever

SYMPTOMS: Sudden high fever, severe headache, joint and muscle pain. Less often, nausea, vomiting and a rash that appears three to five days after the fever begins.

AFFECTED AREAS: Tropics including Southeast Asia, Central and South America, Kenya, Somalia, Mozambique, Angola, Burkina Faso.

MOSQUITO FEEDING TIME: Several hours after daybreak; late afternoon until dark.

RISK: Small unless epidemic is in progress.

Japanese Encephalitis

SYMPTOMS: Most infections cause no symptoms; however, the disease can be fatal or cause central-nervous-system damage.

AFFECTED AREAS: Summer and autumn: Bangladesh, Burma, China, India, Japan, Cambodia, Korea, Laos, Nepal, Thailand, Vietnam, eastern USSR; rainy season: southern India, Indonesia, Malaysia, Philippines, Singapore, Sri Lanka, Taiwan, southern Thailand.

MOSQUITO FEEDING TIME: Dusk, evening.

RISK: Low; danger is greatest among those spending prolonged periods in areas where the disease is widespread; avoid pig farms, rice fields.

Malaria

SYMPTOMS: Fever, flulike symptoms (chills, headache, achiness, fatigue).

AFFECTED AREAS: Large areas of Central and South America, sub-Saharan Africa, the Indian subcontinent, southeast Asia, the Middle East, Oceania (the South Pacific islands including Australia and New Zealand).

MOSQUITO FEEDING TIME: Between dusk and dawn.

RISK: Highest in rural areas but varies markedly from region to region; ask your travel agent or local health department about the risk in any area on your itinerary; consult your doctor about what, if any, preventive measures should be taken before leaving for malaria-prone areas.

PREVENTION: The drug chloroquine may be prescribed or your doctor may recommend carrying a treatment dose of the drug Fansidar to take should you contract any type of fever during the trip and not have immediate access to a doctor or hospital. Chloroquine can produce some minor side effects: upset stomach, headache, dizziness, blurred vision, itching. Fansidar can cause severe skin reactions including itching, redness, rash, mouth or genital lesions, and sore throat; these reactions can be life-threatening but the risk is low: one death per 11,000 to 25,000 users. Discontinue Fansidar immediately if any of the symptoms listed above occur.

OTHER INSECTBORNE DISEASES

African Sleeping Sickness

INSECT: Tsetse fly.

SYMPTOMS: Fever, rash, skin lesions, lethargy, confusion. Symptoms occur six to twenty-eight days after infection.

AFFECTED AREAS: Tropical Africa between 15 degrees north and 20 degrees south latitude.

PRECAUTIONS: Flies are attracted to moving vehicles and dark, contrasting colors; they can bite through light clothing, so wear heavy clothes that blend with background colors; use insect repellent containing Deet (N.N. diethylmetatoluamide).

Tickborne Encephalitis

INSECT: Ixodes ricinus ticks.

SYMPTOMS: Fever with central-nervous-system involvement.

AFFECTED AREAS: USSR, northern Europe from April through August; forested areas. Humans also can become infected via unpasturized dairy products from infected animals.

PRECAUTIONS: Spray exposed areas of skin and clothing with insect repellent containing Deet (N.N. diethylmetatoluamide); avoid tick-infested areas and consumption of unpasteurized dairy products.

Plague
(BUBONIC PLAGUE)

INSECT: Fleas *(y. pestis)* that live on rodents.

SYMPTOMS: Chills, fever, enlarged lymph nodes, confusion, delirium, poor coordination.

AFFECTED AREAS: Widespread areas of South America, North Central and southern Africa, Iranian Kurdistan, along the Yemen–Saudi Arabian border; Central and Southeast Asia.

PRECAUTIONS: Vaccination is recommended for those who plan to live and work in plague-infested areas; risk is small to visitors to urban areas.

Schistosomiasis

INSECT: Larvae of certain freshwater snails.

SYMPTOMS: Occur two to three weeks after exposure and include fever, loss of appetite, weight loss, abdominal pain, weakness, headaches, joint and muscle pain, diarrhea, nausea, cough.

AFFECTED AREAS: Brazil, Puerto Rico, Saint Lucia, Egypt, sub-Saharan Africa, southern China, Philippines, Southeast Asia.

PRECAUTIONS: Avoid swimming or wading in fresh water in rural areas where sanitation is poor. Seawater is safe. Those who suspect they have been exposed should see a physician for testing.

SPRAINS

Any athletic activity can result in sprained ankles, an injury to one or both ligaments on the outside of the ankle. Sprains can also occur in the arms or legs. Symptoms include pain, swelling and bruising. If a leg or ankle is sprained, the victim may not be able to walk. In some cases, symptoms don't appear until hours after the injury.

- Stop and rest.
- Apply an ice pack as soon as possible.
- If a leg or ankle is injured, elevate above the level of the heart.
- If the wrist, elbow or shoulder is injured, place the affected arm in a sling.
- Get medical attention to confirm that the injury is a sprain and not a broken bone.
- Unless you have an adverse reaction, take aspirin or ibuprofen to relieve pain and reduce inflammation.

GLOSSARY

▼

ALLERGY—Immune system response to ordinarily harmless substances among susceptible individuals.

ALTITUDE SICKNESS—Condition believed to stem from change in air pressure and oxygen availability at heights of five thousand feet or more.

ANAPHYLAXIS—Severe, potentially life-threatening allergic reaction.

ANGINA—Chest pain due to insufficient blood flow to heart; also referred to as angina pectoris.

ANTHRAX—Bacterial disease affecting cattle and sheep; transmissible to humans.

ANXIETY ATTACK—see Hyperventilation.

BAROTRAUMA—Bleeding from eyes and ears; caused by rapid expansion of compressed air upon arising from deep water.

BASEBALL FINGER—Torn tendon in finger due to sudden force from throwing or hitting a baseball.

BENDS—Condition caused by air bubbles of nitrogen forming in blood from deep water; also called Caisson Disease, Decompression Sickness.

BUTTERFLY BANDAGE—Bandage shaped like butterfly used for holding cut together.

CAISSON DISEASE—see the Bends.

CPR—Cardiopulmonary resuscitation; combination of mouth-to-mouth resuscitation and chest compression to restore breathing and heartbeat.

CHEST COMPRESSION—Component of cardiopulmonary resuscitation; involves pressing on sternum to restore heartbeat; also see CPR.

CHLOROQUINE—Drug used to prevent malaria.

CONVULSIONS—Violent, spasmodic contractions of arms, legs, body and head; can occur as result of epilepsy, injury, fever, illness.

CYANOSIS—Lack of oxygen; legs and fingernails turn blue; sign of impending suffocation during asthma attack; requires emergency medical treatment.

DECOMPRESSION SICKNESS—see the Bends.

DIABETIC COMA—Loss of consciousness among diabetics due to high blood sugar and excess of acids in the blood.

ECTOPIC PREGNANCY—Pregnancy that develops outside uterus, usually in fallopian tubes; life-threatening emergency requiring surgery.

FANSIDAR—Drug used to treat malaria.

FROSTBITE—Frozen body parts due to exposure to cold temperatures.

HEAT CRAMPS—Muscle pains due to heavy sweating during strenuous activity.

HEAT EXHAUSTION—Heavy sweating; fatigue; clammy, pale skin; headache, nausea; vomiting; muscle cramps; fainting among those unaccustomed to hot weather.

HEATSTROKE—Dangerous rise in body temperature (above 106° F); red, hot, dry skin; rapid, strong pulse; sometimes confusion or unconsciousness; potentially life-threatening.

HEEL SPUR—Injury to connective tissue on bottom of foot due to overuse, improper shoes, running on unyielding surface; also called Plantar Fasciitis.

HYPERVENTILATION—Breathing more rapidly than normally in response to tension or emotional upsets; also called anxiety attack.

HYPOGLYCEMIA—Low blood sugar; also see Insulin Reaction.

HYPEROSMOLAR COMA—Loss of consciousness among diabetics due to high blood sugar; differs chemically from diabetic coma; requires emergency treatment.

HYPOTHERMIA—Chilling of body due to exposure to cold temperatures or wet, windy weather.

INSULIN REACTION—Low blood sugar among insulin-dependent diabetics due to too much insulin, too little food or imbalance between food and exercise.

IPECAC—A preparation to induce vomiting; available over the counter at drug stores.

MOUTH-TO-MOUTH RESUSCITATION—Technique to restore breathing among victims of injury, heart attack or other sudden physical collapse; component of cardiopulmonary resuscitation (CPR); also see CPR.

PLANTAR FASCIITIS—see Heel Spur.

SCHISTOSOMIASIS—Illness transmitted via larvae of certain snails; contracted by swimming or wading in fresh water in certain tropical and subtropical areas.

SEIZURE—see Convulsions.

SHIN SPLINT—Athletic injury to lower leg.

SHOCK—Drop in blood pressure and other internal changes that can lead to death following injury.

SNOW BLINDNESS—Sunburn of eye's surface from reflection of ultraviolet rays on snow.

STATUS ASTHMATICUS—Severe asthma attack requiring emergency medical treatment.

STRESS FRACTURE—Hairline cracks in foot or lower leg due to sudden stress or repetitive motion like running; common among athletes.

SWIMMER'S EAR—Ear infection contracted by swimming in unclean water.

SWIMMER'S ITCH—Intense itching caused by penetration of skin by cercariae, a wormlike species found in water.

TENDINITIS—Injury to tendon due to repetitive motion; common among athletes and the physically active.

TENNIS ELBOW—Injury to tendon in elbow due to poorly performed backhand swing; similar injuries occur among those who play other racquet sports and golf.

TOURNIQUET—A bandage or similar item twisted tight around limb to stem blood flow from wound.

WHIPLASH—Injury to neck and upper spine when body is thrust forward and then jerked back upon impact during automobile accident.

GENERAL INDEX
OF EMERGENCIES

▼

ABOUT THE AUTHOR

PAULA DRANOV is a free-lance journalist who often writes about health, fitness and medicine. She has contributed to many national magazines, including *Cosmopolitan, The Ladies' Home Journal, American Health, Savvy, Woman, New York* and *Lear's*. She has also been a Washington correspondent for the Newhouse National News Service covering health and consumer news, and has held various editorial positions with United Press International.

NOTES

....
....
....
....
....
....
....
....
....
....
....
....
....
....
....
....
....
....
....
....
....
....
....
....

....
....
....
....
....
....
....
....
....
....
....
....
....
....
....
....
....
....
....
....
....

....
....
....
....
....
....
....
....
....
....
....
....
....
....
....
....
....
....
....
....
....
....

NOTES

....

....

....

....

....

....

....

....

....

....

....

....

....

....

....

....

....

....

....

....

....

....

NOTES

....
....
....
....
....
....
....
....
....
....
....
....
....
....
....
....
....
....
....
....
....
....
....

NOTES

....
....
....
....
....
....
....
....
....
....
....
....
....
....
....
....
....
....
....
....
....